MW00592202

simplify your life

a step-by-step guide
to better living

Odette Pollar

MJF BOOKS
NEW YORK

Published by MJF Books
Fine Communications
322 Eighth Avenue
New York, NY 10001

Simplify Your Life
LC Control Number 01-130248
ISBN 1-56731-434-1

This edition published by arrangement with Conari Press.
Book Design by Suzanne Albertson

This book was previously published under the title *Take Back Your Life.*

Manufactured in the United States of America on acid-free paper ∞
MJF Books and the MJF colophon are trademarks of Fine Creative Media, Inc.

QM   10 9   8   7   6   5   4   3

Contents

Foreword by Lillian Vernon   vii
A Life Worth Living   ix

SECTION 1 | **Where Are You Now?**

1 Living on the Balance Beam   3
2 Identifying Choices   11
3 Family Matters   17
4 The Money Pit   29

SECTION 2 | **Getting Time on Your Side**

5 Stressed Out   39
6 Scheduling and Planning Your Time 49
7 Setting Priorities and Managing Time 57
8 Managing Yourself   63

SECTION 3 | **Overcoming Barriers**

9 Saying "No"   73
10 The Perils of Perfectionism   79
11 Delegation: The Key to Growth   87
12 Procrastination: Conquering the Inner Demon 97
13 Decision Making   103

SECTION 4 | **Getting Organized**

14 Organizing Your Home   113
15 Files and Paperwork   125
16 Moving You and Yours   135
17 Life After the Balance Beam   147

Afterword by Barbara Hemphill   151
Resources   153
Acknowledgments   157
About the Author   158
Your Feedback   159

Foreword

In 1951, when I was a young housewife expecting my first child and starting my business, there never seemed to be enough hours in the day to juggle all my responsibilities. Odette Pollar's useful tips would certainly have made my personal life less stressful and my business life more productive. Now, forty-eight years later, I no longer have the pressures of raising a family or launching a company, but life can still seem overwhelming and, at times, difficult to manage. Thankfully, *Take Back Your Life*—a road map through life's complexities—can help you regain a sense of balance and simplicity and increase your appreciation of what is important and most rewarding.

As I read the opening paragraphs of Odette's book, I found myself nodding in response to her questions "Is your life in overdrive?" "Are you simply running out of time?" and agreeing with her statement "You cannot be all things to all people, nor satisfy everyone's needs." But recognizing that one's lifestyle is stressful does not necessarily bring awareness of what steps are required to bring that life back into balance. My friends and professional associates, who I might add are always operating at full throttle, are the same people who, by virtue of their superhuman pace, have not paused long enough to figure out how to achieve a healthy balance between their work and their personal lives. That's precisely where Odette Pollar comes in. In a strong and reassuring voice, she reminds us that the demands of work, home, and self can all be met without sacrificing important values or limiting yourself to an overly restricted lifestyle. In fact, by following her advice and practical action steps, a simplified and streamlined life becomes an *enriched* life—one filled with the things that really matter and with more time and energy to enjoy them.

The solution, which *Take Back Your Life* makes so clear, is to simplify, reduce complexity, and finally, to do less. Odette is not suggesting that you sacrifice what is truly important to you, as so many of us already do, but rather that you assess your situation, determine what is out of kilter, set priorities, and remove those drains on your time and energy that do not add significantly to your life. Best of all, the result of the reassessment will be a life consistent with your essential values and rich in everything that's important to you. It will be a life not measured in possessions or milliseconds but rather in terms of the deep and genuine fulfillment it provides. It is a life worth living, and it is within your reach.

—Lillian Vernon
author of *An Eye For Winners*

A Life Worth Living

Is your life in overdrive? Are the times when you feel a general sense of satisfaction at the end of each day getting more rare? Are you simply running out of time? If so, you are not alone. Combined with our ever more complex personal lives, many of us go to workplaces that are rife with dissatisfactions, unrealistic expectations, and frenetic changes. Even in the best of employment situations, the pace of change and the exponential growth of information can be the cause of stress, burnout, and a fear that there is no relief in sight. Do not despair. You can make simple and easy changes to break the cycle of running frantically just to continue falling behind. The trick is to make a conscious, concerted effort to do less by simplifying and reducing the complexity in your life.

Many of the "things" we strive for—a bigger house, a newer car, a second or third vehicle, more toys—do not bring happiness and satisfaction; frequently they only bring complexity and the need for additional work and stress. It is time to redefine success for yourself.

Given all that we have to do, many of us are losing sight of what is quite probably our ultimate goal: to enjoy our lives and, we hope, have fun as we balance personal and professional responsibilities in pleasing and satisfying ways. It is so easy to let your desire for high performance, success, and status drive you into a situation where no matter how much you do it is never enough. If your standards for achievement are so high as to be virtually impossible, you are your own worst enemy. You cannot be all things to all people, nor satisfy everyone's needs.

When your workload increases, your desire to spend time with family, engage in volunteer activities, work in your community, and have time for hobbies remains the same. How do you do it all? The best way to save time is not by speeding up and trying to force more and more into the same blocks of time. The best way to "get it all done" is to do fewer things. It is by trading one item in favor of another. If you feel overwhelmed and under constant pressure, view your life as a puzzle with too many pieces or the wrong pieces. Using this book, you can create a puzzle in which, for the most part, all the pieces fit.

Managing time well is not the only element involved in regaining balance. You must also find purpose, reduce stress, set goals, and simplify your life. Making life choices is not something that can be done quickly. It is not a one-time, one-decision-will-fix-everything circumstance. To make wise life choices, it is important to spend time by yourself and become reacquainted with your natural rhythms and desires. Notice what you run toward and run away from. This takes some doing, especially in these increasingly hectic times. But it is well worth the effort.

This is not to say that wake-up calls don't happen in a single day. You may be sitting in your fifth traffic jam in three days. Or your child is graduating from high school and you suddenly realize that you are looking at a stranger. Or the doctor tells you that persistent malaise is something more serious. Or your best friend moves to a smaller town and now lives a lifestyle that you view with longing and envy. Or your child has been arrested. The wake-up calls are endless. What matters is what you do when you hear the call.

Begin to notice which areas are out of balance in your life and how that affects you and others you care about. Whether you are married or single, you have a family life that also needs tending. Throughout the book, I do mention families, since many people have them. If you are single, your own close social friendships, your romantic relationships, extended family, and your network are your family.

Regaining balance in your life starts with the awareness that something is seriously out of kilter, that you can influence the direction your life takes, and that you are willing to make changes. Being selective about your choices and clear about your priorities is key. It is vital to keep your perspective and establish realistic expectations for yourself both at work and at home. You will be faced with competing demands and will have to make choices, but the results—more time, more leisure, and a sense of satisfaction—are well worth it.

Over the last eighteen years in my consulting work, and particularly in the last ten years, an increasing number of my clients have struggled with these issues. Their experiences were remarkably similar or contained repeating patterns. Almost universally, my clients have been working very hard for professional success and financial stability. However, over time, whether they were successful in their endeavors or not, they found that their lives overall were less fulfilling. This book is a distillation of the advice and experiences that people similar to you and facing the same concerns as you have used to make decisions that result in more satisfying and fulfilling lives.

Keeping the Goal in Sight

Take Back Your Life outlines a five-step approach to making changes that begins with identifying what is important to you and your family. You do have the answers; it just may take time to recognize them. The first step is to analyze where you are now, the second to assess how that differs from your desires. The third step is to identify changes you would like to make and identify strategies for doing so. The fourth is to make a plan and put those action steps in place. The fifth and final step is to unclutter, reduce, and simplify your possessions and responsibilities.

Take Back Your Life is divided in four broad sections: Where Are You Now?, Getting Time on Your Side, Overcoming Barriers, and Getting Organized. The focus throughout the book is on strategies for managing your non-work hours in a way that brings you more happiness, satisfaction, and peace of mind. There is a great deal of information that is readily available about ways to make your work time more productive. Many of us find that we have many more support options and resources for work-related issues than we do in our personal lives.

Each chapter includes a Things to Consider section with ideas to provoke thought and reflection. It is followed by Action Steps, suggested strategies and very specific steps you can take that will make a big difference in how you feel. This practical, how-to process will help you move forward and accomplish your goals. Some Action Steps involve exercises or experiments you can try. The exercises will take time and do require thought, but these are important decisions you are making. Each chapter ends with a set of Tips—quick additional ideas to get you moving.

No matter how complex your life happens to be, you can make changes that will reenergize you and your family. This is a step-by-step process that my clients have found success with, and you will, too. If you follow these procedures and give yourself time to make the transition, you *will* create a life worth living.

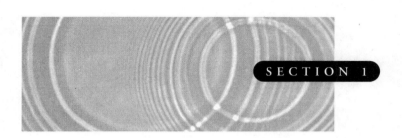

Where Are You Now?

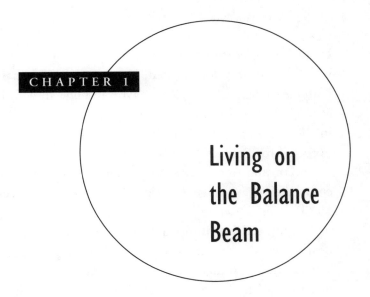

CHAPTER 1

Living on the Balance Beam

These are the days of the time famine. With less time and more demands on your leisure hours, activities like daydreaming, reading novels, taking long walks, or spending afternoons "goofing off" have virtually disappeared. Particularly for the two-income middle-class family, time has become more precious than money. As work pressures increase, more and more people complain that their lives are out of balance, with too much time spent at work and not enough leisure time.

In the "good old days," people had little trouble deciding what to do in their spare time. Leisure time meant just that.

It was an opportunity to do what you wanted, when you wanted, and how you wanted. It was a time to recharge your batteries, relax, take it easy, maybe indulge in a little recreational activity. But things have changed dramatically. Living in the 1990s is rushed and stressful—with more of the same expected for the next century.

According to a Harris survey, the amount of leisure time enjoyed by the average American has shrunk 37 percent since 1973. Over the same period, the average work week, including commute, has jumped from under forty-one hours to nearly forty-seven hours. In some professions, particularly law, finance, and medicine, not to mention entrepreneurship or senior management, work demands often stretch to eighty or more hours per week.

Does this scenario sound familiar? The alarm rings and you jump out of bed. A quick shower (never a bath), and the morning rush to eat (if you have time) and get your family off to work and school has begun. The weekends are no better. Errands must be run, repairs made, cars washed, groceries purchased, and all the other activities required to maintain your possessions and support an active, busy life must be completed. And then there's all the work taken home from the office in an attempt to catch up.

Societal norms and expectations have shifted to support this state of affairs: society now confers status on people who are super-busy. We receive ego strokes, recognition, rewards, and approval from friends and associates for being constantly on the go. Having a calendar jammed with appointments is considered impressive as we live "life in the fast lane." Keeping in touch via beepers, cell phones, and faxes means that work is never far away. Even in our nonwork hours, "busy-ness" is associated with importance. We even rush on our way to exercise, an activity designed to lower our stress levels!

Stress comes from our constant search for ways to do more in a finite amount of time. As work demands increase and intrude on our personal time, more and more people feel that the overall quality of their lives is decreasing. Hence, the ever more frantic search for time-saving products and services.

In our personal and professional lives, we continually try to find those extra few minutes. The rise in popularity of fast food, short hair styles, express banking, and personal computers are all testimonials to our desire to do things faster and more easily. It is safe to say that no one on his deathbed ever wished they spent more time at the office. The trick, when we use labor-saving devices, is to use the time we have freed up wisely. The next time you buy a microwaveable "dinner for two," think about the hour of free time you just gained. Then spend that hour on something really important to you.

Where Are You Now?

The goal in balancing your life is not to try and cram more activities in, but rather to reduce your life's *complexity*. Have you ever felt like an acrobat juggling fragile plates while balancing on an oil-slicked ball that is, in turn, resting on a fast-moving walkway? Do you feel that you are getting older but not any better? Are interesting experiences few and far between? Are weekends simply two days filled with chores and errands and other things you simply must do? Is reading for pleasure a thing of the past?

Running too fast is exhausting. Rushing from place to place, thing to thing, or task to task is not fulfilling. Overstimulation can be as unsatisfying as unwanted isolation.

Do you live in a big city and yet rarely do anything except work? Are cultural and sporting events, outdoor activities, and other amenities of which big cities boast out of your reach—not due to financial difficulties, but rather due to a lack of energy or time? Who wants to brave the gridlocked traffic into the city for a concert, especially after a long commute home from work?

When faced with overwhelming demands, one survival strategy is to shut down—not drop out entirely but disengage emotionally. The minimum gets done. You go to work, care for your children, and keep food on the table, but that is all. The outside world begins to shrink. Your life consists of the inside of a car or train or bus, your office, the store, and the house. Television becomes a focus point when there are a precious few moments before bed. Then you toss and turn as you think about more of the same for the next week, month, or year. Is this your story?

When things are not going well, it is tempting to blame others or rush out and change something—anything—to make the inner pain go away. Radical, unplanned moves often result in disaster. Most of us simply can't or don't want to move to a mountaintop or give up everything we own. And it's not necessary. Rather it's a matter of setting priorities and then creating a life around them. This is a long-term process and requires thoughtful time and insight. You must identify what is important to you, and your partner or spouse must do the same. Children, too, as they get older, should participate in this process. As a way to get started, list three to five answers to these questions:

- When filled, what physical needs make you happy and why?
- What emotional needs are important to you and why?
- What mental needs must be filled to make you content?
- What other needs are important to you?
- What causes the sense of frustration (and perhaps depression) that you feel?
- What does success—both personal and professional—mean to you?
- If you survived a disaster such as an earthquake, a flood, or a fire, what possessions would you miss and why?

From these seeds will come the information that you will draw upon as you begin to build a life that is worth living. Your desires might be similar to the ones discussed by Elaine St. James in her book *Simplify Your Life.* When she and her husband started their simplification program, they wanted the things in their lives, all their possessions, to be small enough and few enough so that they could easily take care of them themselves.

Their second interest was to remove commitments and obligations that interfered with their doing things that they really wanted to do. St. James writes, "For us, living simply meant reducing the scale, maintaining the comfort, eliminating the complexity, and minimizing the time demands of life as we had known it in the 1980s."

You need to reacquaint yourself with your needs, desires

and feelings. This will allow you to identify what you want more of and less of. A plan then will provide you with a systematic approach for achieving your goals.

Things to Consider

Before making changes, consider the results you want to achieve. This will give you a starting point from which to begin to choose a direction and set goals. You might wish to:

- Enjoy work and have enough energy left to enjoy family and outside life;
- Have enough challenge to make work interesting, but enough leisure to keep life in perspective;
- Reduce stress, hassles, and rushing;
- Be able to look forward to your next day, whether it is spent at home, at work, or on vacation;
- Cultivate a better relationship with your children, partner/spouse, or parents;
- Do more of what you want and feel more contentment.

ACTION STEPS

This may seem like a lot of work, but it is time well spent. You need to spend time identifying what is genuinely important to you. Then the rest will fall into place. Otherwise, the time will just get filled up with other nonessentials.

STEP 1   Once a week for two months, sit quietly for thirty minutes and write your answer to the question, "What does a successful life mean to me?" Describe what that will look and feel like. Ask your partner to do the same.

STEP 2   At the end of the two months, take those eight weekly lists and review your answers. Look for patterns and trends.

STEP 3   By reading your answers, identify the most important elements that must be present for you to have a happier life. Develop a single list containing your key elements.

STEP 4   Compare your list with those of your family or partner. Identify and discuss what you would like less of, more of, and why.

STEP 5   Without evaluation, identify many different ways to increase what you want and decrease that which is less desirable.

STEP 6   Repeat Step 5 several times and try to generate a long list of ideas.

STEP 7   Choose those that are reasonable and realistic.

STEP 8   Set priorities and goals for achievement. (See Action Steps in Chapter 2.)

Tips

- Ask for help. Do not let pride or stubbornness hinder you from asking for assistance. Remember that many problems, even personal ones, need not be solved alone. Choose your challenges; sometimes it is not worth solitary teeth-grinding when you could simply ask for help. That might be help with creating a financial plan or completing your tax returns.

- Don't let frustration take control. Set reasonable, realistic goals and actively work toward larger changes. This is a slow process and change will take time. Focus on smaller steps rather than biting off more than you can chew.

- Don't wait for others to make your life interesting. Add variety and new experiences to your life.

- Set priorities. You have to be brutally honest with yourself about who you are and what you really want, and set your priorities accordingly. Getting rid of extraneous activities is one thing, but it is often harder to limit activities that you like but for which you no longer have time.

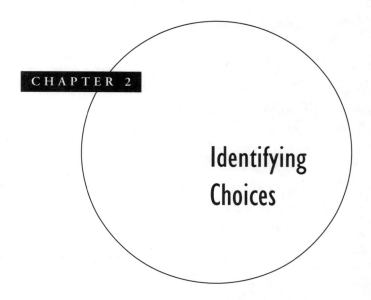

CHAPTER 2

Identifying Choices

F or many, the typical American success story does not provide a satisfying way to live. Constant striving and endless consuming is not worth the cost. When life is filled with meetings, meaningless commitments, cluttered homes, a long commute, and unreasonable work demands, we generally function in a continual state of stress. Trying to have it all can be strangling to your family, your soul, and your happiness. Instead of satisfaction and contentment, you may feel frustration, loneliness, isolation, and a general feeling of emptiness. That is why a trend called *downscaling* is sweeping the nation.

As Dave and Kathy Babbitt write in their book *Downscaling,*

> *Recent surveys document the shift of Americans toward a more relaxed life. Many are opting for a lifestyle that allows time for personal needs, families, and friends—concerns nudged out during the success craze of the '80s when people became so caught up in titles, job descriptions, and salaries that they lost their true identities and work became the thermometer of self-worth.*

> Time *magazine calls the movement back to home life and basic values "pervasive" and says it is evident at all levels of society.* USA Today *dubbed downscaling the "trend of the decade." A* Fortune *magazine poll of working Americans in their twenties found that instead of riches, 75 percent are "more concerned with a rich family or spiritual life, a rewarding job, the chance to help others, and the opportunity for leisure and travel or for intellectual and creative enrichment."*

Many people are reevaluating and rethinking what makes for a satisfying life. Being open to change means reconsidering the status quo. It is not a question of extremes, such as living in a cabin with no running water versus an apartment in the heart of a large city. You will probably find that you don't want to forsake everything you have worked for, but rather you want to find a middle ground. That might mean working in a smaller city that will free you from the commute and rush. You can find many places with the convenience and intellectual and cultural opportunities of big cities, but that do not take over and consume the rest of your life. Where the cost of living does not mean a sky-high mortgage that sucks up your financial resources like a sponge. Where success has a more well-rounded meaning than just moving up a ladder or working eighty hours a week in your own entrepreneurial endeavor.

In simplifying your life, start with easy steps that you can take immediately. Constantly look for ways to reduce and streamline. The following ideas show that you do not have to give up all luxuries or live an austere life. This is not about poverty or deprivation. The object is to make choices and create the time to pursue those choices.

Many Options

If you find it impractical to leave your city, relief can be found by moving a few miles outside the city, moving to a lower-priced area of your town, or to a smaller and lower-priced home. That fourth bedroom, three-car garage, or pool may not really be worth the extra $500 a month.

Even having one day free from your regular commute via telecommuting can have a significant positive result. Friday could be your day to eat breakfast with the entire family, dress casually, and walk to work located in the spare bedroom. A smaller home may open the option for one partner to work only part-time. This is a great opportunity to ask children to help you make these major decisions. Would they be willing to make do with less in exchange for having you home and more available? You might be surprised at the answer.

Adaptations can be made in the way you earn a living or by working a different schedule. Flextime can help you avoid the peak commute rush hours. Perhaps your current employer would allow you to transfer to a less demanding area, department, or division. Could your hours be reduced or could your job be shared?

Another option is to work permanently as a temp. Temporary agencies specialize in placing workers in every type of job category. This is a great way to work regularly and take frequent breaks. The schedule is flexible because you can decide which assignments to accept.

The biggest step of all is to leave the corporate arena and start your own home-based business. There are many resources available to help you get started. While not completely headache-free, if planned well, this can provide the freedom and flexibility you seek.

There are many options, approaches, and strategies. Suspend your immediate inclination to say, "Yes, but," or dismiss an idea out of hand without due consideration. Be open-minded and flexible while evaluating your options.

Things to Consider

The decisions you make are not set in stone. They can change again in a few years if need be. Do not become paralyzed by attempting to make a perfect set of infallible choices.

ACTION STEPS

STEP 1   Work backward from your ideal. Draw a picture of what your ideal life would be like, including:

- Who is in it;
- What type of environment surrounds you;
- What types of activities you are involved in.

STEP 2   What do you have currently that matches this vision? (Probably more of your life than you think is already in alignment.)

STEP 3   Analyze the present situation (cost of living too high, commute too long, not enough family time, too rushed and stressful).

STEP 4   Review the list you created in Chapter 1. Set specific goals and objectives (examples: Reduce mortgage payments $500 per month; reduce debt-to-income ratio to 30 percent; work and live within thirty minutes of home; work only thirty-five hours per week; have time for cultural events; or eat dinner as a family twice a week).

STEP 5   Identify tasks (research work changes, shed volunteer assignments, look for less-expensive housing).

STEP 6   Set a timeline, what will you do and by when. Some can be started within the next thirty days. Some within six months, some may take two years.

STEP 7   Start making changes.

Tips

- Do not worry about fears that lie in the distant future. Focus on issues you need to address today.

- Forge ahead. Understand that anticipation of the worst-case scenario distorts the view of any occurrence.

- Give yourself rewards along the way to celebrate your progress.

- Break things into three categories: (1) some things need to be done better than they've ever been done before; (2) some just need to be done; (3) others don't need to be done at all.

- Check that priority areas are balanced appropriately with your purpose and values.

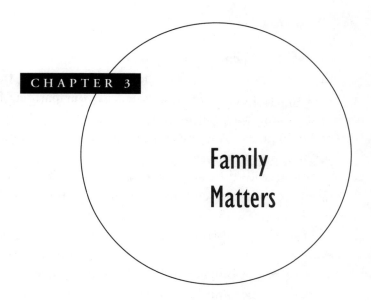

CHAPTER 3

Family
Matters

I n the 1930s and '40s, the word *family* conjured up one image: a husband, wife, and children. Now the definition of family is much broader, encompassing single parents, grandparents raising grandchildren, same-sex couples, unmarried couples living together, and couples with no children. More families are dual-income than ever before. About 77 percent of women with children between the ages of six and seventeen now hold paying jobs, up from 25 percent in 1947, according to the U.S. Department of Labor. No matter what your circumstances, decisions to change your lifestyle will impact the people you love.

Besides a general feeling of malaise, how do you know that things aren't "right"? Is there more squabbling than ever before? Do you feel less interested in your partner? Do you seem to experience entire months of your life without feeling any excitement? Are you so pressed for a spare moment that social opportunities are a burden?

Along with the quest for the affluent life comes the temptation to give our children too much. This might be too much money without responsibility or the understanding of what it takes to earn it. Other children have too much freedom without limits, and when they become teenagers they seem to be out of control. For still others, there is too much pressure to become "somebody," too much food, and too many activities. The overload brings with it physical, emotional, and psychological problems.

In Irvine, a very affluent, conservative city in Southern California, teenagers from wealthy homes began to form gangs. The citizenry were horrified. They thought gangs were a symptom of inner-city, poverty-stricken areas. These Irvine kids joined gangs for the same reasons as their inner-city counterparts—for a sense of control and a need for belonging that they were not getting at home.

Examine the ways you are spending your time in caring for your family. Are important needs going unmet? Kids being ignored or shoved in front of the television set? How about time with your partner? Sex? Or perhaps you are giving so much to your family that you are ignoring your own needs for time alone.

Resentment, hostility, and feelings of unfairness are signals that personal needs are not being met. Your feelings and experiences are valid, and the first step on this journey is to acknowledge them. Before making any firm decisions, it is equally important to learn how the rest of your family is feeling. Whether you accomplish this at a regular sit-down weekly meal, a family meeting, or a one-to-one conversation, lasting changes cannot be made without everyone participating to some degree. After all, slowing down means that all of you will be cutting back, and we hope, spending more time together.

Things to Consider

Recognize the social context in which work and family stress occurs. How much of what you feel is truly caused by having too much to do or by some vague feeling that you ought to do more, be more, or have more?

Examine the source of your guilt. Is it the belief that you are hurting a loved one by what you are doing or failing to do? Examine your beliefs closely. Decide if your concerns are appropriate or unfounded.

Consider the way in which you set limits both at home and at work. Are your expectations of yourself, your partner, and other members of your family realistic?

ACTION STEPS

STEP 1   Meet with your family to discuss their issues, needs, and concerns.

STEP 2   Share your feelings. At this phase, simply talk about the situation, share goals and needs. Just get everyone's thoughts on the table. Save judgments and evaluations for later.

STEP 3   Schedule another time to meet and talk about what to do. Give everyone a chance to think first before jumping immediately to strategies.

STEP 4   At the second meeting, bring paper and colored pens. Write up everyone's ideas. Break them into three groups: (1) Things to be done immediately; (2) things that need more research or information, and (3) things to consider.

STEP 5   For those items that require research, involve the entire family by asking each member to be responsible for gathering some of the information. For example, the kids in the Brown family were finally allowed to have a puppy. Each child was asked to go to the library to find out what breeds are friendly to children, easy to train, and protective but not dangerous. Once the larger issues were resolved and a puppy brought home, the kids took a vote on the puppy's name and divided responsibility for its care.

STEP 6   At the next family meeting, be prepared to evaluate ideas and create a plan to achieve goals.

Tips

- Decide on responsibilities for you and your partner and switch off on tasks either weekly or monthly. For a morning routine, one partner might dress the children while the other makes breakfast. This is easily determined by who has the most patience early in the morning. Who handles a specific item should be decided during a calm time.

- Once a week, give kids lunch money. The break in routine can be fun for them, a rest for you, and teach them how to keep track of money.

- Balance hard time with soft time. Hard time is going to parks, museums, aquariums, arcades, and movies. Soft time is spent together in quieter pursuits, looking at tide pools, reading out loud, taking a walk, talking, riding bikes, cooking, and just generally hanging out.

- To reduce that feeling of never having time for spontaneity, do not make social plans for more than two weekends each month. Give yourselves the luxury on some weekends of having no plans and no schedule to keep. If you feel like enjoying an activity, you can always choose to pull something together.

- Use commute time for storytelling and talking with young children. Traffic conditions permitting, children have your full attention during these times.

- Find ways to occupy your children after school hours. The *San Francisco Chronicle* reported that Geline Molochko, a dental practice manager in El Cerrito, California, did not want her twelve-year-old son coming home to an empty house after school. So she convinced her boss to hire him for tasks like filing and taking out the trash. "He learned about work and responsibilities and was treated seriously as an employee," Molochko said. "He learned more about me and my job, and I was able to keep an eye on him after school."

- When decisions affect the family as a group, make them together.

Have a Great Morning

How do you start your day? Is it a rush from the moment the alarm rings? If you have children and a spouse or partner, is it a mini-Olympic competition to get everybody out the door and onto buses, planes, or trains on time? Some people rise, drink a leisurely cup of tea, exercise, read the mail, and then are primed to face the day. Which are you? To get your day off to a calm start, do some early planning.

The Night Before

Tips

- Evenings are generally less pressured than mornings. Decide what you are going to wear the next day and make sure it is presentable before you go to bed. You can even do this on the weekend and prepare the entire week's wardrobe. Gather items that need to be taken to work or school and put them in the same place every morning. Make lunches, fill bottles, and lay out children's clothes the evening before (folding and storing outfits together is a real time saver). Iron any clothing that requires it.

- Keep things by the door. Always keep your keys, brief-case, purse, and children's papers and carrying cases near the door. Keeping them there eliminates the last-minute frantic search throughout the house for misplaced items.

- Set a time each evening to go through papers from school or childcare and review permission slips, assignments, and party invitations.

- Collect items for the next day and do general straightening of the house before bedtime. This can be a calming routine. It is also pleasant to wake up in serene surroundings. The less you have to do to get started in the morning, the better.

- Plan your breakfast the night before and do any preparation work then. Set the table, put out cereal or fruit, and set the coffeemaker on a timer. This will prevent that blank stare into the open refrigerator door.

- Keep a family calendar and check it each evening, so that the Little League game or the delivery to a neighbor does not catch you unaware. Think about the next night's dinner so any items can be picked up during the day or on the way home.

- Let your children help as much as possible. Older children can make their own lunches as well as perform some chores around the house.

- When you know a morning will be particularly rushed, put small children to bed in sweats or soft play clothes so you need not change them before daycare.

In the Morning

Tips

- Put a clock in the bathroom.

- Consider getting up earlier than the rest of the

household. This is a way for you to have some calm, peaceful, quiet time for yourself.

• Give yourself enough time to wake up, get ready, eat, and leave for work or drop the children off. If this time is ample, you can spend it mentally preparing to start your day. Cutting things too closely or getting up at the last minute means you start your day rushing and run the risk of being late. You will expend a great deal of energy before you even arrive at the office.

• Give yourself an extra ten or fifteen minutes of unscheduled time. It is a mystery, but occasionally the daily routine of taking a shower, brushing your teeth, and dressing will take longer for no discernible reason. A little extra time is also helpful for dealing with the inevitable accidental spill or tear.

• Unless you are expecting an important call, do not bother to answer the phone when it rings. You are already on a tight deadline and the last thing you need is a sales call. Never forget, the phone is there for your convenience, not for the convenience of the caller.

• To cut squabbling about who gets into the bathroom first, allot a specific time for each person.

• Encourage everyone to do some of his or her grooming in their bedrooms. Hair dryers, curling irons, makeup, and the like can be stored and used near a mirror in the bedroom. This frees up the bathroom for tasks, such as showering or teeth-brushing, that cannot be done elsewhere.

• If you take your children to school or daycare, let

them choose a special activity they can do if they get out of the house on time, having collected their own materials. It might be a quick detour to the park for ten minutes on the jungle gym, being read a story before leaving, or getting to choose the radio station in the car.

- Keep pocket change in a bowl for last-minute needs, calls, school lunches, parking, tolls, and the like.

- A good treat for older children, if they are ready for school on time Monday through Thursday, is to take them to the local café for a quick breakfast before school on Friday.

- Resist the urge to do that "one last thing" before walking out the door. Leaving by 7:15 means walking out the door at 7:15. This does not mean hooking up the dishwasher, trying to find the keys, or writing a quick note. All of those things that will "only take a second" actually consume minutes and make you late. One special danger, if you have children or a childlike adult, is turning on the television. It takes real discipline to turn it off precisely when you need to.

Keeping Romance Alive

Amid the flurry of daily activities and responsibilities, finding time to nurture and grow your relationship with your partner can get pushed aside. Family needs on top of work demands makes things even more difficult. At the end of an exhausting day or week, you may only have enough energy to sleep. Here are some ideas just for the two of you.

Tips

- At least once a month make a dinner date with your significant other. This is special time for the two of you. Make sure you choose a place where you can sit and talk and really focus on each other without other distractions.

- Develop a hobby that interests you both. Taking a cooking class, joining a choir, ballroom dancing, or exercising together are good ways to bring new experiences into your life, meet new people, and broaden your horizons.

- Make it a point to schedule time for intimacy until your life is in better balance and you can be more spontaneous. Keep romance alive by making it a priority. If you and your partner always get into bed exhausted, the days and weeks will fly by without much contact.

- Stop working nights and weekends. When extra effort is unavoidable, make it a rule to not work on Sundays or to keep two evenings work-free each week.

- Share chores and errands. If one partner is primarily responsible for doing most of this work, by the time it is completed, he or she will often be too tired for romance or much of anything else.

- Teach your children to respect your quiet times and privacy. If you have a home office or a workshop, children must learn that playing there is unacceptable. Teach them that when the bedroom door is closed, they must knock before entering. If all else fails, install a lock.

• Occasionally go to bed thirty minutes or one hour early and take some time for each other. Leave the television set off.

• Schedule a long weekend away together at least once every three months. Alternate the person responsible for planning the dates or long weekends. As a surprise, consider making the plans a "secret" until the weekend arrives.

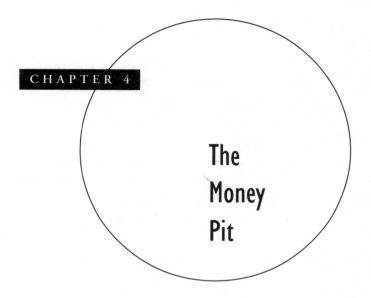

CHAPTER 4

The Money Pit

S hopping has become a national sport: consumption as entertainment. Western society says that enough possessions will fill all needs, including emotional and spiritual ones. There is a definite correlation between the accumulation of things and your frenetic lifestyle. The more you spend time acquiring, the less time you spend evaluating the necessity of your purchases. How often have you bought an item, brought it home, and then lost it? There was so much other "stuff" that it got misplaced. Or, while you were looking for something else, have you come across a purchased item you forgot all about? Did you really need it in the first place?

It is easy to get caught up in consumerism. Quick, get the newest model. Bigger is better. More is better. The advertising field thrives on creating the appearance of need where none exists. Purchasing mania is a spiral that makes it incredibly easy to get overextended. How easily we forget that possessions cost time and money and require maintenance. One of the beliefs of the '80s was that the more you earned, the more you bought; the more you owned, the more services you could purchase that would help make your life simpler and easier. You may have had a different experience. How many of the following do you have?

- Gardener
- Cook
- Housecleaner
- Chauffeur
- Fashion consultant or personal shopper
- Bookkeeper
- Personal fitness coach
- Hairstylist
- Shopping service
- Baby-sitter

This is only a partial list. Some households have a more extensive staff than do small businesses. The scheduling logistics alone are enough to make your head spin. Do people show up when promised? Is the work always up to par? How often do you have to find a new service provider? Is it really easier to live a life where you, in effect, manage a household staff and a team of consultants?

Scaling back your lifestyle is realizing that success is not measured in tangibles but is a process of investing in the intangibles of daily living. Relationships are what matter, and having time to develop and nurture those relationships is important.

As Dave and Kathy Babbitt write in *Downscaling,*

> *Downscaling is about margins and limits. We abuse financial limits by living beyond our income. We abuse physical limits by not getting adequate rest nor eating properly. We abuse our emotional limits by subjecting ourselves to more and more stress.*
>
> *Our society has helped us by providing a set of peripheral industries to deal with stress, time management, financial planning, and debt consolidation. Instead of setting rational limits, we hire services to help us continually live beyond them.*

Living a simpler life is not about deprivation. It is about moderation and control. If you have what you need, have control over your spending, are out of debt and have a nest egg, you'll have a great feeling of security. That's better than a new toy any day. Simplifying is a chance to appreciate what you care about and focus on what is truly important.

Personal Choice

Where does your time go? Ask yourself on the next lovely Saturday when you would prefer to be outside but are stuck balancing three bank statements, justifying five or more credit card bills, trying to remember which expense should be written on which account, "How is it truly more convenient to have accounts spread out over town?"

It is easy for investments to become complex. Do you have mutual funds from one source, stocks from another, and bonds from a third? Not only do you have to deal with the account statements along with promotional material, but your tax preparer also has to reconcile dividends and gains at the end of each year. Are you really getting enough additional earnings to justify the maintenance time?

Consolidate most of your investments into a single fund. You can always diversify within the same family of funds that you choose. The key to financial success is consistency. Save and invest year in and year out. It is not how much money you make, but rather how you spend it that makes the biggest difference in what you have and how you enjoy it.

Personal fiscal responsibility is learned. Teach children early about money: what it is and is not good for. Make sure they realize the importance of saving. Kids need to understand that they cannot have everything they see. Some items are not affordable and so tradeoffs must occur: the bicycle or the tennis shoes, but not both.

And there is no law that says that a current need must be met by a new product. Consider an item that is used, refurbished, or simply an older model. Divorce usefulness from newness. You might not need a new version of some items (camping tents used twice a year, for example). I bought refurbished office furniture because it served the purpose, was in excellent condition, and I realized I would only need it for three years. It was much more economical than an identical-looking new set.

Older versions or editions of products may often work better than new ones that seem to be designed to wear out. My parents received a toaster as one of their wedding gifts. That very same toaster was passed on to me and now is being used by a family friend. It has not stopped working or in any other way ceased to function as it was designed. My mom gave the toaster to me when she bought a new one that would accommodate bagels. The first "new and improved model" broke after five years and she is now on her second new toaster.

Things to Consider

- Before buying an item, ask, "Do I need it or simply want it?" If you need it, ask a second question: "Is there anything I own that, with adaptation, can do the same thing?"
- Change your buying strategy:
  - Designate one day a week for shopping;
  - Ask how long you will use a new item;
  - Resist the temptation to buy the first one of an item that you see. Walk away and think about it before purchasing;
  - Delay major purchases for a set amount of time. Do you still want it in one month?
- Have the courage to ask for a better deal, particularly on high-ticket items. Often you can get a better price just by asking.

ACTION STEPS

STEP 1   For one month, keep a list of every expense you have. Keep a notepad in the car for those quick coffees and other easily forgotten cash expenditures.

STEP 2   Sit down and figure out how much you owe.

STEP 3   Create a reasonable budget that allows you to pay your bills and provides some luxuries but not an excessive number. How austere a budget is based on how out of control your situation is.

STEP 4   If you need help, get advice from a debt counselor, accountant, or bookkeeper, or read books on debt management.

STEP 5   Set up a savings plan as you pay off your bills. Automatically save 10 percent or 15 percent of your income each month. After that becomes comfortable, say in six months or in one year, save an additional 10 percent.

STEP 6   Look for ways to economize. Taking lunch to work three days a week versus going out combined with cutting one evening restaurant dinner could easily save $100 a month. Without much sacrifice, you would have $1,200 at the end of the year. That could easily buy two round-trip tickets to Europe.

Tips

- Carry only one credit card and pay it off every month. Why carry more and pay more than one annual fee or have additional checks to write each month? And remember, those interest payments are astronomical.

- Collect and pay bills twice a month only. For cash flow purposes, you may choose not to mail the payment until closer to the due date, but a system makes the chore much easier.

- Create a system for manual bill paying. Keep stamps, envelopes, return address labels, the checkbook, and a calculator close at hand. When a bill arrives, open it, place it immediately in the return envelope, attach a return address label, note the due date on the outside of the envelope, and put it in a tickler file. At bill-paying time, write the check, enter it into the ledger, put the check in with the bill, file the receipts, and mail it.

- Have as many bills as possible converted to automatic payments by your bank. Consider using pay-by-phone or other online services. This eliminates paperwork and saves you postage costs and frequent trips to the post office for supplies.

- To make buying harder, only use cash. Counting out $20 bills feels different than whipping out a credit card. It will make you stop and think.

- Keep track of expenses as they accrue so that tax time is not so onerous. Keep receipts sorted by month and by category.

- To resist impulse buys, do not rely on memory. Make a shopping list and stick to it.

- Do not go shopping as a form of entertainment. If you want to treat yourself consider a host of other activities. Read a book, go for a walk, or visit a museum.

- Learn to record the amount of a check in your check register *first*, then write the check.

- Do not renew a subscription to a magazine you don't have time to read. Once your schedule is free, you can resubscribe.

- Shop around for the lowest price, but not to excess. Saving $5 is not worth the drive across town, parking, and waiting in line; saving $50 probably is.

- Schedule actual appointments into your calendar for managing financial tasks.

- Give consumable or experiential gifts, such as gift certificates, food items, tickets, or overnight stays at local spas. You will help your friends avoid excess possessions, and it is much easier than finding something that your friends or relatives (particularly if they are an older couple) do not already have or need. Giving a donation to a charity in their names may be greatly appreciated.

- Establish a special fund for unexpected expenses.

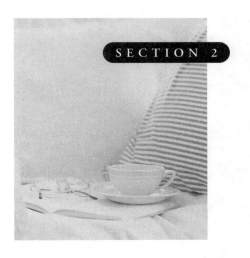

SECTION 2

Getting Time on Your Side

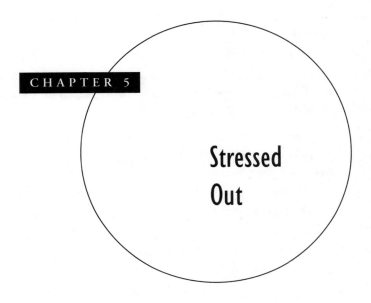

CHAPTER 5

Stressed Out

A project deadline has been moved forward. An unexpected visit from the main office requires your presence at a dinner tomorrow evening, knocking out your plans to attend your child's recital. Two key players were unavailable for a meeting, which instead of being canceled was held anyway to no purpose. Your car has developed a strange knocking sound when you accelerate. Your favorite necklace broke as you were getting dressed, and you now must get it restrung. And it is only Tuesday.

Constant deadlines, shorter response times, and more demands have created ever-increasing stress levels for most of us. According to "The Mitchum Report on Stress in the '90s," conducted by Research and Forecasts, Inc., most Americans say they experience "some to a lot" of stress in their daily lives. Fear of losing their jobs, the pressures of marriage and family, fear of crime, environmental concerns, and difficulties making ends meet are just a few of the day-to-day worries facing workers in these very turbulent times. "Stress is an epidemic now," asserts Don Powell, president of the American Institute for Preventive Medicine, a behavioral health consulting firm in Farmington Hills, Michigan. "It's more pervasive now than perhaps at any other point in our country's history."

Trying to excel at work and at home can make you feel as if you are caught between a rock and a hard place. Your personal and professional responsibilities seem overwhelming, and the more you do, the more others demand. The need to achieve can drive you to stretch your resources ever thinner, and in the end, you can become trapped in a self-perpetuating stress cycle.

Living at a fast pace without a way to relieve the pressure will cause stress. The more tightly choreographed your life, the more likely an unexpected problem can throw off the day, week, or month. Not having a clear day in your schedule for three or four months in advance probably indicates that you have too much to do.

Stress is not always a bad thing. You need some amount of stress to perform effectively. Too little stress can be as harmful as too much. The trick is to manage stress and not allow it to manage you.

Stress comes from positive experiences like getting married, starting a family, a new job or a cross-country move, as well as from negative experiences like divorce or the death of a family member. When channeled constructively, the additional surge of energy, concentration, and excitement triggered by imminent danger can spur you on to greater levels of productivity and creativity. That tension helps you strive and try just a little harder. When the speed and pace of daily life is fast, even occasionally overwhelming, but you can still cope, your stress level is manageable. Stress has gotten out of hand when the pressure is unrelenting and you begin to feel demoralized or backed into a corner. Without relief, this energy-draining mobilization can lead to health problems ranging from headaches to heart attacks.

Many high achievers feel they must be everything to everybody and tend to expect too much of themselves. When goals are either unattainable or irrational, the goals not only foster a sense of inadequacy and failure, they become "set ups" for feelings of unworthiness. The unreasonable expectations of high achievers are wired to their self-esteem, causing them to continue to strive for the impossible instead of changing their standards. Examine whether you are putting unnecessary pressure on yourself due to unrealistic expectations of what you can and should do.

Managing Your Response

Reducing the stressors in your life is ultimately the best way to prevent problems. Often your own perception of a situation, not the events themselves, makes the difference between feeling either anxious or unperturbed. The way you interpret situations influences whether your body resists or succumbs to stress. Researchers of health-related issues generally agree that people who feel a sense of control experience stress positively, while those who feel powerless tend to respond to pressure with anger, depression, anxiety, or other harmful symptoms.

When your feelings build up without relief, you will experience strain that can eventually cause mental and physical exhaustion. What is stressful, tension causing, anxiety producing, and hard to deal with for you may not be for your best friend. This is why the advice to "just not worry about it" is easier said than done. We all react to situations differently. Learning to handle stress and dissipate the tension it causes helps keep us mentally and emotionally fit in the same way that exercise keeps our physical body fit.

You can learn to cope with stress and stressful situations with a little practice. It is realistic to learn to manage it better but not to try to eliminate it entirely. No matter how much you try, you cannot control every external cause or source of stress. The best thing you can do for yourself, therefore, is to be aware of how you react to stressful situations. Learn to recognize when you need a period of relaxation, whether it's five minutes or a two-week vacation.

Remember that you can't change the way other people react or behave. It is futile to rage against them. If you find yourself frazzled because other people don't behave the way you wish they would, a healthy coping strategy is to work on changing your responses or to avoid the situation in the future. The traffic congestion is not going to get better any time soon. Becoming irate at a driver who merges poorly or tailgates certainly drives your blood pressure up, but it doesn't affect the other driver. Recognize that poor drivers exist and that you should expect to encounter them occasionally. Do not let yourself get so upset at someone else's seeming stupidity.

Recognize when you have the leverage to change a situation and when it is clearly beyond your control. At work, you may notice one supervisor who seems to respond more quickly to problems presented humorously. You might discover the fun in figuring out how to present a problem with levity. Your goal is to get the problem solved; if that can happen pleasantly, so much the better.

Your thought processes have a great deal of influence on physical symptoms. Changing your response patterns fall into three areas:

1. Change your internal attitudes/perceptions:

    • Talk about your troubles and feelings with friends and family;

    • Learn to see the humor in difficult situations;

    • Maintain a social life, but not one so active that you feel forced to "have fun;"

    • Seek professional counseling if necessary to help through difficult times.

2. Change your environment:

    • Remove distractions and noise;

    • Stop attending functions that take you away from your family too often;

    • Change jobs, careers, or work location;

    • Remove clutter.

3. Change your physical ability to cope:

- Exercise regularly;
- Engage in relaxation exercises;
- Get adequate sleep and rest;
- Take regular vacations or shorter three- and four-day mini-vacations;
- Eat well. Proper nutrition is important.

Things to Consider

Those of us who are chronically stressed out usually hold certain unconscious assumptions. Are any of these beliefs true for you?

- I have to do things perfectly.
- I should be able to do more in each day.
- I function best under pressure.
- It is important to please others by doing what they ask of me.
- I am invaluable at work; no one can do as good a job as I can.
- I can do it all and have it all.
- Once I have it all, I'll be happy and life will be wonderful.
- Relaxation is my reward, but only after I get everything else done.

These attitudes lead us into disappointment as others expect more and more of us. We may feel tired, frustrated, and angry toward family members, friends, bosses or coworkers who do not recognize our self-sacrifice as we strive to do the impossible.

ACTION STEPS

STEP 1   Answer the question, "What is the right balance for me between work, rest, and play?"

STEP 2   Identify areas in your life that cause you harmful stress.

STEP 3   Take those areas you listed and break them down more specifically. For example, it is not your children specifically who cause stress; it is

- When they tell you about school assignments the night before they are due;

- When they have sporting events and obligations every evening of the week.

STEP 4   Consider how long a particular situation will continue. Will it stop in two and a half months after summer ends? And, can you live with that? If so, great, but be sure to decide what will you do next summer so the situation does not recur.

STEP 5   Identify simple changes that will ease your schedule. Read the newspaper before the toddler awakens or schedule one less errand each day.

STEP 6   Discuss with other parents how they manage similar stressors.

Tips

- Say "No" with regularity. Constantly being too busy is often caused by saying "Yes" to everybody else's priorities, and thereby saying "No" to your own.

- Do not substitute caffeine, sugar, or tobacco for sleep. When you are tired, you are in no shape to cope with stress.

- Break up recurring patterns that cause stagnation. Break up routine, dull weekend activities by doing something new and exciting at least once a month. Make your weekend and vacation activity the opposite of the type you have at work. If your job is slow and predictable, your weekend can be more fast-paced. If your job is too fast-paced, take the time to vegetate at home.

- Loosen up. Be more playful. Take yourself less seriously. Everything is not a pivotal moment in history. Once your emotional reservoir is empty, it is hard to shrug off little stressors.

- Take a fifteen-minute break in the morning and in the afternoon. Move around to get the blood flowing. Weather permitting, go outside. The change in scenery, not to mention the fresh air, will help you divert your attention from stress-producing concerns. This is a positive distraction that will help you return refreshed to tackle the issues.

- Keep a reminder to slow down. Little reminders can be as simple as a blue dot sticker on the computer or a small note on the phone to take a breath before answering.

- Use deep-breathing exercises to help reduce tension. When you are tense, your breathing becomes rapid and shallow. To slow down your breathing, inhale naturally, but exhale long and slowly. You will probably feel your shoulders return to their normal position.

- Take a break from frustrations, deadlines, and high-tension situations by eating your lunch away from your desk. Do not skip lunch altogether.

- Exercise is important. Aerobic conditioning helps you weather stressful situations with fewer physical and emotional effects because it reduces the intensity of the stress response. Most people think they are too busy to exercise regularly. The good news is that twenty minutes of exercise four times a week is very effective. No matter how busy you are, you can probably squeeze in a twenty-minute workout somewhere in your day.

- Let your needs be known. No one else can read your mind. Assert yourself by clearly presenting your feelings to others. This helps release pressure and avoids the build-up of negative or harmful emotions.

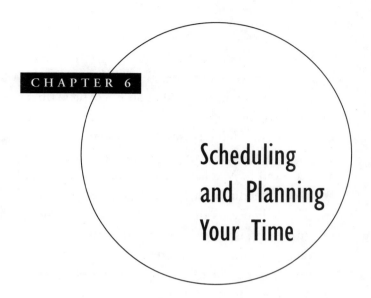

CHAPTER 6

Scheduling and Planning Your Time

D o you face each new day with a low-grade case of panic? How are you going to fit everything in? If your mornings start in a rush, the pace does not slow during the day, and your evenings are jammed with activities, your schedule is out of control. One symptom of an overloaded life is a schedule jammed with commitments. Social opportunities are often seen as obligations when you are overscheduled. When going out with friends seems more of an assignment than a fun thing to anticipate, it is time to sit back and reevaluate what really matters.

If your calendar is literally bulging at the seams, one consequence is never feeling caught up or in control. In the continual rush from task to task, you never have time to breathe, or to stop and appreciate what you have accomplished. Overcrowding detracts from the specialness of each activity.

Time is limitless, and scheduling is a way to put boundaries around it. Managing your schedule requires planning in advance. Scheduling helps you gain control over the flow of routine daily events that make up your life. One of the goals of simplifying is to have fewer things that call out to you and distract you from your desires.

To make any of the changes discussed in this book, you need a plan. How are you going to accomplish the changes you want to make? It is tempting, particularly if you are fed up, to grab for any change just so long as something gets better. Try to avoid rash decisions like jumping up and moving across country "just for a change." The result is likely to be the same situation, just in another climate. The plan you outlined in chapter 2 will serve as your overall guide. Now you must make sure that you are moving daily toward your goals. Sometimes a simple, easy change is all you need. If adding exercise to your busy day is important, but there never seems to be enough time, be creative. If you eat dinner thirty minutes earlier, the entire family could take a half-hour walk after dinner. It is lovely to be out during the longer summer evenings. You not only get exercise, but also quiet, undisturbed time with your family.

Chronic Lateness

One challenge is to create a realistic schedule so that you do not find yourself continually late. It is uncomfortable to always be rushing, having to apologize, or sitting in traffic fuming at other drivers who are delaying you. Are they really the source of your problems? Here are some strategies for combating chronic lateness:

1. Your internal clock, which provides you with time-related information, may be set a little fast. You underestimate how long it will take you to drive somewhere, gather the information, or pack. The easiest way to remedy the situation is not to try to reset your clock. Learn, rather, how far "off" it is, then always add that amount of time to whatever your internal estimate says. So, for example, if you are chronically late, add an additional fifteen minutes to your internal estimate. Some people even find it helpful to set their watch ahead by that much.

2. Even though you are generally late to arrive, do not feel that things cannot change. Teach yourself to think differently. Begin to see yourself as someone on time instead of saying, "My parents were like this, too," or, "Oh, late again. Well, they expect me to be late anyway." New messages that counteract this are very useful. Think of a person you like and respect who is on time. What does he or she do? Imitate that.

3. Be prepared, so that you won't have to look for the keys, locate the sunglasses, or brush your teeth at the exact moment you need to leave in order to catch the bus.

4. Start eliminating some of the excess tasks and responsibilities from your life. Being late can be a way of rebelling—a way of saying, "Oh yeah, you can make me attend, but not participate or be on time." If you have too much to do, begin to cut back. Volunteer less, skip a season, and say "No" more often, even to little things.

5. Be aware of grandiose thinking, such as believing that you can squeeze thirty appointments into a day, do all the fund-raising for that special event in four hours, or arrive at Chicago's O'Hare Airport on Friday afternoon at 3:30, retrieve your luggage, and get downtown in time for a 4:30 meeting.

6. If you are a chronic overbooker or overextender, estimate the time to perform each item on your To Do list. Then add it up. Add 20 percent extra for the unexpected. That's really key; so much of what gets people off their schedule is not planning for the unexpected.

You may find that you simply do not have enough hours in the day for everything you think you need to do. Consider those constantly accumulating little things that never seem to go away. These often necessary but low-payoff activities can suck up all your time, preventing you from getting your important items done. Put those routine items under scrutiny by asking whether you can save time without sacrificing results by doing one of four things:

1. Change the frequency. Save up items for the cleaners so you make fewer trips and select a cleaner that is closer to your home.

2. Reduce quality standards. Dust less often or allow a quickly thrown comforter to comprise a made-up bed.

3. Adopt new methods. Learn quicker or easier ways to clean household items or allow dishes to air dry rather than manually drying them.

4. Delegate. Ask your teenager to take the family car to the car wash, to pick up cleaning, or do other brief errands on Saturday mornings.

Openness to new ways of doing routine tasks more efficiently will allow you to dedicate more time to worthwhile endeavors, such as attending your eight-year-old's Little League games or getting exercise at the local swimming pool.

Things to Consider

A schedule is a tool to help you manage your life and commitments. It should not be a millstone around your neck. If you need lots of freedom and open, uncommitted time, then schedule to accommodate that need while still having time for the mundane, routine tasks, such as laundry, that must be done to keep your life running smoothly. Total chaos is not freeing.

ACTION STEPS

STEP 1   Make a chart and list of all of your responsibilities. One list for work and one for your family. Be as thorough as you can.

Task/Responsibility	Must Do	Ought/Should Do	Would Like to Do

STEP 2   Look hard at the *"Must Do"* items. We often assume we need to do more than is actually necessary. Try to move some into the *"Ought/Should Do"* column.

Step 3   Look at the *"Ought/Should Do"* column. If you completed everything there would you have time for the *"Would Like to Do"* items? If not, ask these questions about your task list:

- Is it urgent or important?
- Can I delegate it?
- Can I be more flexible about how I accomplish it?
- Can I change how I do this in the future?

Step 4   Be creative in answering these questions. You will find a wide variety of choices and options available to you.

Step 5   You can't shed everything at once. Make some decisions on your list and start now. After a month, review this list and make a couple more changes. Do this until your schedule becomes more manageable and realistic.

Tips

- Don't confuse long hours with productivity; they are not synonymous.
- Always look at your schedule before agreeing to accept new work or responsibilities. In order to add something, you must eliminate something else from your schedule.
- Set aside time every week for important priorities that require blocks of creative time. Plan your day around high-payoff activities. You need to schedule time for

longer projects and not allow returning phone calls and other routine activities to eat up all your time.

• Track multiple projects for all family members on a wall chart. Use a different color for each member of the family. Post it in a easily reachable place.

• Consolidate similar activities such as answering telephone calls, correspondence, bill paying, and errands, and do them together.

• Build routine activities into your weekly pattern of life. Back up your computer every Friday, pay bills on the first and the fifteenth of the month only, change the beds on Monday, and replace batteries in smoke detectors every New Year's Eve.

• Schedule the next appointment for the dentist, doctor, or beautician before leaving their office.

• Do not make appointments for every open slot in your day; leave some spaces open because things inevitably take longer than you think.

• Schedule multiple appointments for the same day instead of spreading them throughout the week. This reduces your travel time and parking hassles.

• Buy greeting cards for occasions like birthdays, anniversaries, get wells, and thank yous at one time so that you need not make special trips.

• Use checklists to help do routine things more easily and quickly.

• When meeting with busy people, ask for the first appointment of the day. Your chances of having to wait are reduced.

- If, knowing what you know now, you would not have gotten involved in a particular activity, begin to look for ways to drop it.

- Keep a copy of your warranty or repair information in your tickler file on the anniversary of the item's purchase date. Once a year, most warranties are up for review, and routine service calls can be placed at that time.

CHAPTER 7

Setting Priorities and Managing Time

How you manage your time equals how you live your life. Making choices based upon priorities allows you to invest your time in such a way that your desires come to pass. Setting priorities is a matter of making decisions about the relative worth of tasks, people, and projects that are clamoring for your attention. There is always something you *could* be doing. Something always needs to be cleaned, straightened, or repaired. It is never ending. You cannot find more time for yourself without making changes and setting limits. Setting priorities, planning, and scheduling are at the core of any successful time management program.

The heart of the matter is how you manage tasks within the same twenty-four-hour timeframe that is available to everyone. Your life should be fulfilling. And that is possible with some planning. Plans relate directly to your mission and goals and provide a road map to follow. Without plans, you are easily sidetracked. Do not resist planning by letting common misconceptions, such as the following, stand in your way:

• It takes too much time.
• The best-laid plans go awry, so why bother?
• I value spontaneity and planning is too inflexible.
• Only boring people plan all the time.

It is not necessary or even advisable to plan every second of the day. The object is to plan the important activities on a daily and weekly basis. Consistency helps ensure success. Haphazard planning produces haphazard results.

Clearly, we all must do things that we wish we didn't have to do. With clear-eyed vision, you will be surprised to discover just how much choice you have about where your energies go. Remember, you really do have the capacity to make choices. And that is the key to your simpler life!

Use this chart to help you identify the choices you make and help you zero in on options. Complete the chart by identifying all the tasks you do regularly. This is another way to look objectively at all of the things you commonly do. Be very creative about finding options for handling some (not all) of the tasks.

Task or Activity

Task you are doing	How long does it take?	Can anyone else do it?	Satisfaction level	Role expectation	Can I live without it?	What would replace this?

As you examine your activities and weigh the pluses and minuses of a different approach to any or all of them, take a look at your relationships with people.

How would you evaluate the quality of your relationships? Do you spend enough time with the people you love and care about? Relationships are one of the most important areas in your life. They need to be examined regularly. You may need to spend less time with those who do not matter so much in order to spend more time with those who do. You interact with many people; just be sure the time investment is appropriate for your:

• Neighbors

• Associates

• Acquaintances

• Relatives

• Family

• Friends

• Coworkers

Weed out people who truly waste your time, drag you down, or give you a pain. It is harmful to keep them in your life if they give nothing in return. Friends are important to your overall happiness, and spending quality time with them is critical. So is making new friends.

Expectations can be opened up to the light as well. Free yourself by eliminating some of the "shoulds" and "musts" in your beliefs. There is very little that you absolutely, hope-to-die, must do. The rest is all choice.

Rigidity makes most of us unhappy and causes excess stress. Being open to new ideas, situations, and experiences can give you an opportunity to experience more and learn more. Is there really only one right way? Must all meals be eaten at the dining room table and breakfast food eaten only in the morning? Is the vacation ruined if one thing goes awry? Be more flexible and open. Shaking things up, every now and again, is healthy.

Think in terms of options or choices. A wide gap, not a fine line, exists between being flexible and being spineless or wishy-washy. Feel free to hold your ground on important things, but how much really deserves the table-pounding?

Things to Consider

When times or circumstances change, revise your plans accordingly to fit the new conditions. Rather than abandon them, revise with a focus on creativity and an action orientation.

ACTION STEPS

STEP 1   Take your weekly schedule and add two columns, one labeled *"Priority"* and the second labeled *"Time."*

STEP 2   Set priorities on every listed task and identify how much time you think each item will take. Add up the *time* column for a total.

STEP 3   Compare the list to the want list you created in chapter 1. Is there anything from your want list on your schedule?

STEP 4   Add one thing to your weekly schedule from your want list.

STEP 5   If your allotted time is already gone, reevaluate your task list with a view to eliminating some. Which others can be done less often, less well, or by someone else?

Tips

• Volunteer to do something only after you give up something else. Do not add unless you subtract.

• It's so easy to leave leisure for last, and then not get any at all. When planning for the upcoming month, season, or year, schedule vacations, family time, and key social events first. That will force work to adjust around the schedule.

• Set a time limit for boring or overwhelming tasks. They will seem less onerous if you know you can stop soon.

• Competency is seductive. Do not spend a lot of time on things that are not important just because you are good at those activities.

• Use drop-off and delivery services as much as possible. When you add up the time it would take to drive to the service, park the car, deliver the document, and return to pick it up, it is probably more expensive than having it sent to you.

- Spend more time with friends. After all, these relationships are very important. When you review your life, it is the friendships and your experiences, not the number of telephone calls you returned or meetings you attended, that will be the measure of your success.

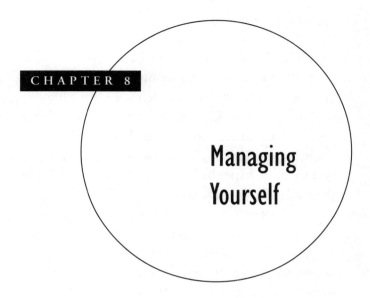

CHAPTER 8

Managing Yourself

I n the best of times, with today's demanding pace of work and life, the level of sustained energy required to meet expectations can be hard to maintain. Particularly if you are in a customer service or public contact position, pouring your all into meeting client demands can take its toll. The phone never stops ringing, and there is always another issue to deal with or question to answer. In situations where stress rises but never seems to lower, and catching up daily becomes more unlikely, you may find yourself getting depressed. If you then go home to a chaotic environment, with months of deferred maintenance and another busy weekend, the constant pressure will take its toll.

To take care of other people, you must first take care of yourself. You have probably noticed that if you wait to take care of yourself in the time left over after handling all your other responsibilities, you are often the loser. If you are waiting for recognition for all your hard work or permission to slack off, you will wait in vain. A change won't occur until you make it happen. It is crucial that you set time aside in your calendar just for you and guard it jealously.

What's wrong with setting 3 to 5 P.M. Saturday for a long stint in the garden or 9 to 11 P.M. on Monday evening to read? Start with a two-hour block of time for yourself each week and gradually increase it over time until you are feeling more in balance.

Reevaluate your habits and traditions. It is not slothful to have a less-than-perfect home. Once enjoyable activities become performance endurance tests, it's time to reevaluate. Expectations that are too high and inflexible become traps. If meeting a high standard on a social activity—hosting the perfect party, having an immaculate garden, or creating a picture-perfect holiday season—gives you a sense of satisfaction, that's great. But once the standard becomes a burden, the joy is gone. If it leaves you with too little energy to enjoy the activity or other areas of your life, it's time to relax your standards. The key is to identify the cause of your malaise. And while you are at it, take a look at your habits.

The way you manage time is often based on habit. You do what you do because you have always done it that way. Habits are unconscious behaviors that are automatic. Habits that were once helpful can get in your way when your situation, environment, or job changes. Changing your old behavior patterns can help you manage time more effectively.

Creating New Behaviors

Psychologist William James suggested an approach to changing habits that is quite effective. He recommended that you do the following:

1. Launch the new behavior as strongly as possible;

2. Seize the first opportunity to act on the new behavior;

3. Never let an exception occur until the new behavior is firmly rooted.

Launch an exercise program by announcing your plans, creating a workout schedule, asking for help in keeping you on the straight and narrow, and sharing your experiences. Make an announcement to your family or fellow car-poolers that you will no longer go ballistic at examples of incompetence shown by other drivers. The very next time a driver offends you, ignore the offense, laugh at the offense, turn on the radio instead, but remain calm. Act on the new behavior that you have promised you will engage in. Until the new behavior is firmly rooted, do not let an exception occur. Three to four weeks is usually enough time to break an old habit and replace it with a new one.

Other psychologists have studied behavior change and discovered that simple habits can be broken in about twenty-one days. Follow these seven steps to launching a new behavior and watch the transformation:

1. Identify the new behavior;

2. Think about ways to practice the new behavior with gusto;

3. Publicly announce the new behavior for a strong beginning;

4. Do the new behavior every day for twenty-one days consecutively;

5. Post signs to help remind you of the new habit;

6. Be willing to feel slightly uncomfortable until the new behavior takes hold;

7. Change the environment to reinforce the new behavior.

If you've decided to stop going to the local pub for a beer after work on Fridays, let your drinking buddies know that you not be going with them. As an alternative, try going to the gym or library, or make a social date with a friend you have not seen in a long while.

Changing habits takes time and energy. Desire and determination are the keys to success or failure. Be diligent, at least in the first three weeks. Try not to deviate from your new behavior until it is firmly rooted. Beware of crises. When a crisis hits, you are likely to swing into action automatically, reacting in the old ways you know best. Once in a crisis, your attention is on the immediate problem, not on your new routine. You may push everything else aside and lapse into the old automatic behavior. If you do find yourself slipping, simply go back to the new behavior and start the twenty-one-day cycle again.

Be aware of the things that trigger or cue your habitual behavior. Cues are trigger events. Most behavior is a response to stimulus, such as getting hungry at the sight of delicious food. Recognize what triggers the behaviors you want to change. Once you have the trigger event identified, you have three ways to approach habit change: change the trigger event, change your response to the trigger event, or change both.

Things to Consider

The only person who can manage you is you. Resist the temptation to assign blame and relinquish control over your ultimate happiness to others.

ACTION STEPS

Step 1   Think about a behavior you successfully changed in the past. How did you feel about that accomplishment? How did you do it?

Step 2   Select one habit you would like to change.

Step 3   Follow the seven steps outlined on pages 65–66.

Step 4   After three weeks, evaluate your results.

Tips for Home

- Seek calmness immediately before and after work. Restructure your morning routine so that it is relaxing. See Chapter 3 for tips on how to do this. It may be reading the paper early, listening to music on the way to work, or eating a leisurely breakfast.

- Stay motivated. If you find affirmations and motivational quotes helpful, post a few where you will see them often each day. Similarly, listening to motivational tapes during your commute can help the transition from work to home. Unwinding before arriving home allows you to move into the rhythm of home life more easily.

- Walk regularly with a friend. It is a great way to maintain relationships and get exercise.

- Make time for your hobbies. When work is particularly draining, it is important to do something you enjoy. That balance helps offer a more realistic perspective on the workplace. Fill your leisure time with rewarding things that have value for you.

- Keep a list of fun activities and be sure you do at least one each month.

- Slow down a little. Meditate, add a few minutes as a cushion to your commute, or delete one task from your To Do list. Give yourself time to breathe.

- Purchase event tickets together with friends. Plays, movies, concerts, and other outings are great ways to appreciate cultural events and share experiences.

- Schedule a regular "grown-ups" night out; keeping it on the same date each month (for example, on the fifth or the second Friday) makes it easy to remember.

- Get an annual checkup; whether you are feeling good or not, it's preventative. You change the oil in your car regularly and the water in the fish tank, don't you? You deserve at least the same amount of care.

- Watch your diet. Good health is easier to maintain than to regain.

- Sleep enough each night. Sleep deprivation and the resulting tiredness is insidious. Develop a relaxing evening routine before bed to encourage sleep.

- Keep a pad of paper and pen by the bed for quick

notes. Or, use a tape recorder for work issues. Once safely noted, you can get or return to sleep.

• Only take on what you are able to do and are interested in. Finish what you start before jumping into something else. If you are a person who is constantly captivated by new ideas, use a folder to contain them and tell yourself you will look at it as soon as you finish what you are working on.

• Do not feel obligated to answer the telephone every time it rings. Get rid of the call-waiting feature. Is it really so important that you not miss that call? Unless you are officially on call, most things can wait the few minutes until you are off the line.

• Don't rely on your memory—write things down.

Tips for Work

• Focus on the positive. Try to keep your day's work in perspective. There is always good news; it is just often overwhelmed by the next problem. Make a commitment to notice and comment upon one good thing that happens each day.

• When you are feeling isolated, talk with coworkers. Whatever problems you are experiencing, they probably are also. Talking things over is often helpful and will make you feel better. If you share complaints, do not forget to spend some time talking about the positive so that you leave your conversation on an up note.

• Do not bother to use your time to learn something you really do not need to know or will not use more than once. Get help and move on to things that are more valuable.

- Focus on praise when you receive it. You probably get kudos more often than you realize and dismiss it with a "Yeah, but" statement.

- Never take the work personally or let your self-esteem suffer. When a customer complains, it is not about you or your family. Remember their frustration is based on their expectations of the company which were not matched by what occurred. You just happen to be the one who answered the phone.

- Don't take problems home. When you are at work, be there 100 percent, but leave it when you go home. Worrying about what is left on your desk or what might be upcoming just destroys your ability to rest and refresh yourself. Remember that whatever comes the next day will come with or without your worry and agony.

- Use the stairs rather than the elevator for short hops. As you become more comfortable, increase the distance. It serves as a daily workout. As part of your regular routine, it is convenient and takes no additional logistics, and—considering the slowness of elevators and the number of stops—it is often faster.

- Beware of micromanaging issues and frittering away energy on little things.

- Celebrate your accomplishments. On your way home, reflect on the tasks you completed during the day and be pleased with how much you did accomplish.

SECTION 3

Overcoming Barriers

CHAPTER 9

Saying "No"

Have you noticed how requests for your time are always couched as benefits or presented in a way that strokes your ego? Helping to raise funds or give a speech will provide so much exposure. Serving on the board will give you leadership opportunities or increase your standing in the community. Chaperoning the kids' outing will help give you time outdoors. Please help because you are the best planner and Roberto's retirement party deserves the best. We need your guidance on, could you help with, you are so good at.... The requests go on and on.

Some are not even direct requests, but rather assumptions that you will take on the responsibility. Expectations can be quite insidious. Suddenly, jobs fall onto your plate unnoticed. Who decided it was primarily your responsibility to manage, shop for, and run interference with your in-laws? Participate in the extended family, certainly, but how did the birthdays of his or her mother, father, kids become your entire responsibility?

Not saying "No" when you need to do so is a real trap. Are you guilty of being more sensitive to the needs of other people than you are to your own? Why is it so tempting to shift your priorities to the back burner in favor of meeting everyone else's requests? Are any of these underlying reasons true for you?

- Being helpful makes me feel needed.
- I was taught that saying "No" is rude.
- I'm so much more fortunate than _____. I ought to help out.
- I feel guilty when I say "No."
- They won't like me if I say "No."
- I like the image of myself as a person who can juggle all these things. It boosts my ego.

Saying "Yes" too often piles more burdens or obligations onto your already overflowing plate. Other people won't respect your limits until you learn to set them from the very beginning. From where does that extra time come to "help out"? Usually, from your rapidly disappearing free time. Watch for the trap of magical thinking. The belief that you will (somehow, magically) "have more time later." Next weekend always seems so much longer than last weekend.

To begin saying "No" more often, think through the request, look at your schedule, and evaluate your interest, desire, ability, and time. Review the request in light of your priorities, some of which are based on who really counts in your life. To what activities would you like to donate your energy and experience? Remember, to keep life sane, you have to be willing to say "No" to something if you say "Yes" to something else.

This is not to say that helping others or donating time to worthy causes should be avoided. These can be noble and satisfying. They only become a problem when doing so will take away time from other important areas of your life. Decide where responsibility to yourself begins and your responsibility to others ends. Keep in mind that a "No" is simply the refusal of a request for you to volunteer your time. It is not a personal rejection of the other person or a reflection of their self-worth or importance. Honoring your time and your earlier, previously given promises is simply a matter of respect—respect for yourself and your commitments. It is better to be wholeheartedly involved when you do agree to help out than to become overextended and feel resentful toward the request, the requester, and the project.

Saying "No" appropriately is also better than coming back later and reneging on your agreement. This leaves the requester in the lurch and feeling resentful toward you, which leaves you looking much worse than if you had said "No" initially, allowing them to find someone else. Here is a four-step process for saying "No" that, with practice, will become easier:

1. Listen to the request in its entirety to make sure that you understand what is being asked of you.

2. Say "No" immediately. Do not be tempted to justify first, or offer a slew of excuses. If you are thinking "No," say so right away without hesitation.

3. Give reasons. The explanation should be short and about you, for example, "I already have a prior commitment." "I do not have any free time." "I can't take on anything else right now." Avoid accusatory comments, such as, "You are always coming to me, why not try someone else?" This tactic will only produce arguments.

4. Offer alternatives. Help the other person find alternative ways to solve the problem or meet his or her needs. Perhaps you can be available at a future date. You might be able to accommodate part of the request but not all of it. Offer the name of another person, group, or organization that could be of assistance.

Things To Consider

What is the worst thing that will happen if you don't make everyone completely happy 100 percent of the time? You and your needs and the needs of your family are as important as other people's—maybe even more so. Remember: Guilt is not fatal.

ACTION STEPS

STEP 1   Think about situations you have faced recently when you wanted to say "No" but did not.

STEP 2   Practice saying "No" in situations that are safe— those that do not have a lot of emotional charge to them.

STEP 3   For ticklish situations practice how you will say "No" to the requester in advance with a friend. Practice sounding comfortable and confident.

STEP 4   Say "No" at the very next appropriate opportunity.

STEP 5   Congratulate yourself. Focus on the other things you will now be able to do.

Tips

- To refuse requests, use a buffer, such as an assistant, partner, or friend who can pass along your refusal. "Quan asked me to call you back today so there would not be any delay. As much as she would like to participate in the retirement party planning, she is already committed on Thursday evening."

- Never agree before checking your calendar. If an immediate answer is required, say "No." If you are unsure, say, "I need time to think about it. I will get back to you tomorrow if I can participate."

- If face-to-face refusal is too difficult, offer to call the person by the end of the day with a decision. Then say "No" firmly and without guilt. With any luck, you will be talking to an answering machine.

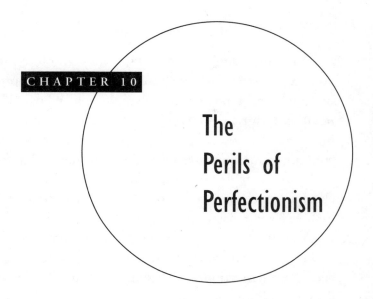

CHAPTER 10

The Perils of Perfectionism

"Katherine is such a perfectionist." Depending on the intonation, these words can be a high compliment or an expression of exasperation. When it carries a positive connotation, it implies high standards and a keen attention to detail. The flip side of this behavior is less positive. An insistence that things be "just so" can irritate friends, family, and lovers. Perfectionism is often coupled with a strong tendency to obsess about things and be overly compulsive. This is unproductive, frustrating, and often unhealthy. There is a high price to be paid for perfectionism.

Without a doubt some tasks require absolute precision. Your cover letter and résumé certainly. A surgical procedure or your final jump for the Olympic gold medal. The final manuscript for a book (any mistakes you find in this one are intentional). However, lining up paper clips, redrafting a common e-mail message eight times, or measuring from the edge of the table to center the candles does not require absolute precision. Perfectionism can waste time and cause high levels of tension for no appreciable outcome.

A ten-year study of over 9,000 managers, completed in 1994 by Human Synergistics, found that 18 percent of managers were perfectionists. They had a 75 percent higher incidence of illness than did their better-adjusted office mates. Their tendency toward perfectionism did not stop at the office door. If you are that way at work, you are likely to be the same at home.

Traits

How can you tell whether you are a perfectionist? If you are, or someone you love is, this will sound familiar. Perfectionists have difficulty in recognizing when enough is enough. What can be described as "reasonable performance" is never quite good enough. Any job can always be improved, particularly with hindsight. How much extra time do you spend polishing things that, if you were to be ruthlessly honest, you would admit do not deserve the extra attention?

Perfectionists have trouble establishing clear goals for themselves or for others. Letting go enough to delegate is a real challenge. Giving control and authority to other people and trusting that others can perform to your exacting standards are often sources of contention. Getting bogged down in minute details, checking work at every step of the process, and an inability to give other people the authority to make even minor decisions can be traits of a perfectionist. At home, a less-than-perfect outcome from another person results in either accusations of incompetence or snatching the project back and doing it yourself.

Perfectionists are very hard on themselves and unforgiving when they make a mistake. When others make one, they are equally unyielding. This sometimes causes troubled relationships with colleagues and partners. Rhea Cross, a graduate student at California State University, Hayward, says, "I often overcommit so that I have the opportunity to prove myself, and then when I end up meeting all the commitments it is at great stress to myself. It also takes a toll on my husband because I take my stress out on him."

Many perfectionists actually fear making mistakes because mistakes are not seen as single, isolated events, but as the beginning of a downward spiral that will ultimately lead to complete failure. Wanting to make things perfect protects against the remote chance that a mistake will occur. In the extreme, doing nothing can be viewed as preferable to taking a risk and the potential exposure to failure. So, perfectionists often procrastinate. The longer the delay, the longer they are protected from the consequences of finishing a project.

Of course, it's impossible to live a mistake-free life. The trick is not to avoid mistakes entirely, but rather to avoid making the same mistake repeatedly. Failure is a great teacher. It is both sobering and enlightening. You can learn a great deal from getting it wrong, often more than what you learn when things come easily to you. Every personal success story, from the boardroom to the sports deck, is full of examples of failures, missteps, and goofs. Remember, Thomas Edison tried more than a thousand filaments for the light bulb before he found one that worked.

Perfectionism and the pursuit of excellence are not the same thing. Having high standards is fine, and so is wanting others to perform well. But the trap for perfectionists is the need to prove yourself over and over again. In the long run, how truly important is much of what you spend your days doing? Focus on excellence which is attainable, healthy, and exciting. Perfectionism is destructive, degrading to others, and depressing.

How does one become a perfectionist? As with other behaviors this one, too, is learned. Sometimes it is from a parent who insisted that the children be immaculate at all times. Sometimes teachers instill feelings of inadequacy. Some teachers never praise but are quick to point out faults or spend time with star pupils while slighting the rest of the class. Certainly it can be helpful to track down the cause of this behavior, but it is not necessary. In fact, a stalling tactic can be the never-ending search for the source of the behavior. It's more important to recognize if perfectionism is causing you to be overburdened and overstressed.

Once you identify perfectionism as a problem, simply decide that you are capable of modifying it and begin to take steps to do so. Does your anxiety about things being perfect interfere with the attainment of your priorities, goals, interests, and desires? If so, change it. To the person who says, "But I've been like this for thirty years," I say, "That may be true. But you are going to live at least another forty years. Do you really think you are incapable of learning new things?" Most behavior can be modified. It is not necessary to try for a complete personality makeover.

Things to Consider

Ingrained habits are hard to break, so start slowly. Begin to recognize the difference between an acceptable level of performance and a perfect level of performance. Nobody really likes perfect people. The harder you try to be perfect the more others feel that they do not measure up, creating a losing proposition for both parties.

ACTION STEPS

STEP 1   Select one major area in your life: work, house-keeping, volunteer activities, etc.

STEP 2   Identify the repetitive tasks you do that you feel need to be perfect. Recognize the areas that bring out the perfectionist in you.

STEP 3   Search out those tasks that can be done to a lower standard but still be acceptable. Start by choosing areas with a lower emotional impact for you. As you become more comfortable, tackle the more emotionally fraught areas.

STEP 4   Throughout this process, become aware of extremist thinking: "If it is not absolutely the best, it is terrible." Recognize and appreciate a middle ground. Focus on what you're gaining by relaxing your standards: more time off or increased time with family members.

Tips

- Focus on results. Weigh the value of completed although possibly imperfect work over late but ideal work.

- Set attainable, reasonable goals not only for others but for yourself. Perhaps that means going home earlier in the evenings or stopping on the third draft of an internal memo instead of the sixth. Getting someone else to help you set those new goals is helpful because, if left unattended, your tendency is to overcommit.

- The Rule of Three applies here. By the time you have done something for the third time, it is probably time to let it go and move on.

- Consider the worst-case scenario. What is the worst that will happen if the hem is not perfect? Probably not much. Getting an important letter in the mail in a timely manner is better than worrying needlessly over the margins.

- Let delegation free you from unreasonable standards. As long as someone else does it well, you need not do it at all or worry about doing it perfectly. Ask yourself two important questions: "Which of these decisions can someone else make?" and "Even if their decision is different from mine, is it something I can live with?" If so, let them make those decisions.

- Do not obsess over mistakes. They are opportunities to learn more, not indications of an irreparable character flaw. An insistence on never making a mistake makes learning new things practically impossible.

- On low-payoff, low-priority items, look for the least amount of work you can do and still have the task be considered acceptable.

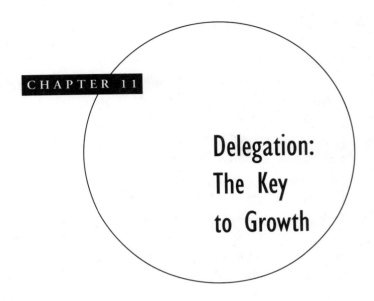

CHAPTER 11

Delegation: The Key to Growth

D o you feel as though you are the only person in your family who can make travel arrangements, choose a physician, or clean the bathroom? Even if you are not a perfectionist, inability to delegate may be part of the cause of imbalance in your life. Have you ever said or thought, "If you want something done right, do it yourself." "I can't afford to pay someone else." "It will take me more time to explain it than if I do it myself." "It's faster and easier for me to do it so I'll take care of it."

Sound familiar? This is a common refrain from people who take on too much and are reluctant to delegate. On a surface level, these may all be true statements. In any single instance, it may be faster to handle it yourself. However, never transferring responsibility to another means that job will remain on your To Do list forever. Initially, delegating takes time. To assign it requires that you clearly define the task, find someone to do it, train the person, and commit to being available to answer questions. Yet, the more you delegate, the more time you gain in the future. Lack of delegation will trap you in the role of constantly doing. You will always have too much to do with too little time left for yourself. Allowing others to participate in completing the work is an excellent way to provide an opportunity to grow and learn. It is a key way for children to learn responsibility. For colleagues and partners it is a way to share the work and avoid becoming overloaded and possibly feeling resentful and discontent.

How can you tell whether you delegate often enough? Here are five questions you can ask yourself:

1. Does your family enter a time warp when you go alone on a trip or a vacation, so that everything looks exactly the same or worse upon your return? Does your family have trouble completing chores unless you are present?

2. When you are away, do you worry about what is going wrong in your absence? Do you secretly feel that disaster is just waiting to strike?

3. Are you still handling the same activities and problems that you did two years ago? Granted that some routine activities and problems are inevitable, but are you caught in a rut?

4. Are jobs stacking up and going undone because you do not have any time to attend to them?

5. Are you continually finding it harder to stay on top of your work because you are involved in too much routine detail?

If you answered "Yes" to most of these questions, it is time to make a change. Delegation is a skill, and you can learn it. As you delegate, you will find yourself with more time for important things. The first step is to lay to rest some common misconceptions. Delegation is not:

• Passing the buck;

• Giving up control;

• Refusing to make a decision by assigning it to another;

• Running roughshod over your family;

• Shirking personal responsibility;

• Dumping unpleasant tasks onto someone else.

All family members within their capacity need to share all the aspects of family life—the fun, the security, the comfort, and the love—along with the mundane chores and responsibilities that keeps everything together. Children are not delicate wilting flowers who are unable to do anything. Unless you are an ogre, requests to pick up toys, do dishes and laundry, and help to make the household run smoothly will not really open you up to prosecution for abuse. Rather, it will take the burden off you while simultaneously teaching your kids responsibility and good work habits.

Steps to Effective Delegation

Effective delegation requires you to do the following:

1. State a clear objective or outcome;
2. Determine guidelines for the project;
3. Set any limitations or constraints;
4. Grant the person the authority to carry out the assignment;
5. Set the deadline for its completion;
6. Decide the best means to monitor the project. This is particularly important for longer projects or in situations in which a great deal rests on the outcome.

When assigning a project, be sure that the person fully understands your requirements. "Clean up the kitchen" means different things to a parent than to a child. Define what you expect. Similarly, be sure that complex projects are fully outlined. Make yourself available to answer any questions, particularly on first attempts.

The person must have the responsibility and accountability for completing the assignment. With teenagers, select jobs that fit their capabilities, but let them have the authority to make necessary decisions and to take appropriate action to complete the assignment. Be sure to set clear boundaries or terms on their authority level, such as, "It cannot cost more than $50 or take longer than two weeks." This could work on anything. Setting boundaries is an important element. For example, the job your child is looking for cannot be farther away than twenty miles or require your child to work past 10:00 P.M.

For longer projects, identify where, when, and how you want to be informed about the progress. Breaking them into phases is a good way to periodically check in and see how things are going. The regular progress reports will let you monitor the situation and make corrections if necessary.

With a partner, you may find yourself negotiating more often about mutual needs and desires. Couples often argue about differing standards on how and when a job is to be done. Be aware if a conflict is caused by a true difference in standards or a case of one partner manipulating the other. Be aware of the dynamics between you. When a great idea for a weekend away on a boat arises, who ends up chasing down companies and making inquiries? Planning, even for fun activities, can still be hard work.

The final component—and for many people the most difficult aspect of delegation—is personal self-restraint. Step back and do not hover. Allow the person freedom. Remember, even though you might start the same project much sooner, it does not mean that he or she must do so. Do not get nervous or make any comments until the first check-in time arrives. If you have a partner who feels strongly about autonomy and independence, this is particularly important.

Delegation is a powerful tool. Every task or project successfully completed builds a greater level of confidence and allows others to handle more and more responsibility. It is a great way for kids to learn responsibility, particularly if you assign projects tied to entertainment or activities they like to do. Why must you worry about the pick-up and delivery schedule for all three older children? Give them the information they need along with any pertinent facts. You may be surprised by their ingenuity.

Trying to get children to help out can become a high-tragedy, operatic scene. Firmness is called for. Doing chores is everyone's responsibility. If you back down it will be even more difficult next time. Children understand consequences. Be clear about your expectations, why the requested chore matters, and what will happen if the garbage isn't taken out each week. Your thirteen-year-old probably won't care that the garbage collectors will miss a pick-up outside. He or she will care, however, if on Friday morning the garbage is sitting on their pillow, as you promised.

Use positive reinforcement. As Stephanie Culp says in *You Can Find More Time for Yourself Every Day,* "Compliment completed tasks, and from time to time, issue positive reminders. Agreeing to a request provides a good opportunity to issue a positive reminder. If your child wants to go to a friend's house for a sleep-over, you can respond, 'Well, you've done such a good job with your chores for the last week—and without being reminded—that, yes, you can go.'"

Things to Consider

What is your underlying fear about letting go? Is it:

- Fear of losing control?
- A high need for perfection?
- Fear of offending others?
- A belief that only weak people need help?
- Fear of a bad outcome reflecting on you?
- A secret desire to play the martyr?

ACTION STEPS

STEP 1   List all the reasons it would be good for you to delegate more regularly.

STEP 2   Identify one small task and one larger task you could assign to another person.

STEP 3   Consider what skills or information they need to successfully take over the task.

STEP 4   Suggest any tools or resources that are available. Explain the task and project. Make sure your instructions are specific and comprehensive.

STEP 5   Let them find their own approach.

STEP 6   Praise what went well often and publicly. Don't be critical initially. They will perform better over time.

STEP 7   Enjoy your extra time.

Tips

- Put aside your worries about infringing on another's time. Your partner's time may be valuable, but so is yours; don't be afraid to ask for, and expect, help.

- Let family members know what is expected of them in advance. If you want your teenager to cut the grass every Saturday, don't wait until Saturday morning to issue an order.

- Get everyone involved. Don't overload the child who always seems to be willing to help.

- Break jobs down into manageable pieces. If children

are too small to thoroughly clean their entire rooms, ask them to put their clothes away or pick up and store their toys. Slightly older children can clear the floor of objects and make their beds. Teenagers can pick up clothes and items in their rooms weekly, do laundry, and vacuum.

- List activities and responsibilities. Write down who is supposed to do what for at least a week at a time. Post it for everyone to see. This way, you can bypass the squabbling over whose week it is to load the dishwasher. Rotate the chores so everyone gets the benefit of learning how to do everything.

- Be aware of sabotage. The spouse who cleans the bathroom once and does a pathetic job of it is likely doing it poorly on purpose. Give your spouse the opportunity to do it over again and again. The same approach works with kids who deliberately do a chore poorly. Learn to live with the sorry results for a few days or a week, then make sure the same person gets the same chore again. Eventually, the person will get the message that sabotage tactics don't work, since he or she will only have to do it again next week.

- Be prepared to reduce your expectations initially. Concentrate on the outcome. A poorly made bed is not as good as a well-made one, but it's better than an unmade bed. Remember, practice makes perfect.

- Resist telling people all the details about how to do something. Instead, tell them what needs to be done and the results desired along with any criteria. Allow them to choose the method.

• Hire help. If you are drowning in chores with not enough family hands to help out, hire someone else or a service to do the work. Even if you only do this occasionally, this investment has a major payoff. You will be buying more time for yourself to enjoy as you see fit. Unless you have no money whatsoever, stop wasting energy worrying about the price for such services.

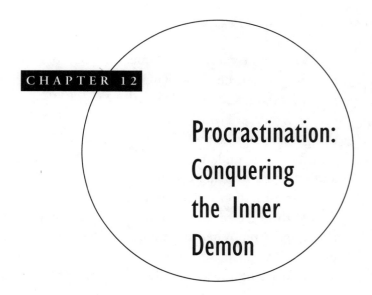

CHAPTER 12

Procrastination: Conquering the Inner Demon

Do you find yourself waiting until the last minute to finish a routine chore? Is getting the information and records together in preparation for the accountant at tax time a hair-pulling, stay-up-until-midnight-the-night-before, nail-biting experience? Is the fence in the backyard still yawing into your neighbor's rose bushes because the summer has somehow disappeared, and who wants to build in the rain and snow of winter? Do you delay starting or completing the most important tasks until you're in the mood, the time is right, or you've finished one last item? You are not alone.

Whether at work or at home, everyone procrastinates at one time or another, to varying degrees. Occasional delay on less important tasks that have no harmful effects to you or others is no problem. However, once the habit of putting things off creeps into all areas of your life, it can wreak havoc on your career, undermine your ability to function effectively, and sabotage your success.

Procrastination is the habitual delay in starting or seeing a task through to conclusion. It is making promises and breaking them. When the time rolls around for starting the project, procrastinators find something else to do instead. The underlying causes of delay are often subtle and subconscious. Combat the tendency to "wait until tomorrow" by recognizing the hooks that can trap you.

The Seductiveness of Delay

Procrastination is seductive because there are short-term positive rewards that come from putting things off. When you have too much to do, deciding not to do any of them can reduce the immediate tension and stress you feel. There is a natural tendency to avoid unpleasant things. Putting them off (even though you will have to do them later) means, at the very least, that you do not have to face them right now. Plus, if you are lucky, they will go away or someone else will do them.

Procrastinating can be exciting. It causes crises and the adrenaline rush that goes along with them. Waiting until the last possible minute is really similar to pitting yourself against the odds. You are gambling that not only will you win out over stress, fear, hunger, and fatigue, but that the mail will arrive on time, the copier will not break, the other person is not out sick, and you will find a parking space as you race to your 10:00 A.M. appointment. When you make it, you probably feel an euphoric high. These are intense feelings, much more so than the quiet, calm satisfaction produced when the project is completed early.

Sometimes fear of change is the culprit. When situations are in transition, you might feel a loss of control. Thus, procrastinating is a way of exerting control over the tasks, projects, or situations that make you feel uncomfortable. You may delay learning a new technology, looking for a new job, confronting a recalcitrant employee, or resigning from a volunteer committee. Since no one can force you to start, delaying slows things down and keeps the familiar around just a little longer. It is a more socially acceptable way to hide your head in the sand than to climb into bed and pull the covers over your head.

Waiting until the drop-dead date to start a difficult task can also be used as a defense for poor performance. You can always claim that it would have been better had there been more time. Delaying can also shield you from the consequences that you expect to occur after the project is completed. For example, choosing to reject a high-visibility committee appointment shields you from the consequences of (1) being in the limelight and possibly failing, or (2) doing well and being offered more challenges than you can handle.

Everyone procrastinates at one time or another, but for some people it's their only approach to getting (or not getting) things done. Even so, the fear and uncertainty that often accompanies new ideas, procedures, and jobs does not have to immobilize you.

If you routinely put things off, the following suggestions can help you break the habit and prevent possible damage to your family, personal relationships, and career.

Things to Consider

Here are some helpful attitudes and new ways to think about procrastination.

- Notice when resentment, anger, or buried rebellion is really the root cause of procrastination. Address the issue directly. Separate the emotion from the task itself.

- Focus on the future. What will be better after the job is finished?

- Give yourself sufficient time to break this habit. Do not decide all at once that you will never do it again. Review chapter 8 on how to change a habit.

- Recognize the greater unpleasantness, work, loss of money, or stress that results from delaying an important action or decision.

- Remember that procrastinating over long periods hurts more than the relatively short-term pain associated with doing any given task.

ACTION STEPS

STEP 1   Do not chastise yourself for past behavior. Be confident that you can change this habit pattern.

STEP 2   On your next project or commitment, set realistic performance expectations for yourself. After doing so, check with another person whose opinion you respect. He or she can confirm that your revised expectations are realistic.

STEP 3   Choose one project and break it into small, manageable parts. Smaller tasks are attractive because they are short, easy, and produce immediate gratification. Keep in mind that all projects, no matter how massive, are only a series of small items reassembled.

STEP 4   Put each small step onto your calendar.

STEP 5   Look for the positive. Stop dwelling on and rehearsing the less pleasant aspects of the job. Create enthusiasm to counterbalance the unpleasantness.

STEP 6   Reward yourself for forward progress. When you have been successful at completing a portion of the project, a reward is a great way to reinforce good behavior. It can be as simple as taking a well-deserved break, a quick walk, reading a few chapters of a book, or getting a massage. For larger accomplishments, rewards might be going to a concert, a weekend "getaway," or a new item you have truly been dying to have.

Tips

• Work with your mood. When you do not feel like doing the part of the project you had planned, find a more appealing aspect and begin.

• Barter the task with someone and do a task for them in exchange.

- Initially focus less on method, technique, or procedure than on your goal of getting important tasks done.

- Do the most unpleasant thing first thing in the morning when you are fresh. Prevent the buildup of fear and dread.

- Start small. Aim for twenty minutes of work on your task. Short amounts of time help maintain momentum. Big tasks do not have to be done in big chunks of time.

- Remove distractions from the environment: close the door, use an empty office, or go into another room.

- Mix up the types of activities the project calls for: planning, talking, researching, writing, for example.

- Identify several starting points. There is rarely only one right way to begin.

- Keep current work separate from your decision about future projects. Stop the cycle of saying, "There is only more work after this."

- Take regular breaks.

- Reward yourself for good behavior. Punishing yourself for goofing off is not nearly as effective. Reward yourself at milestones in the process, not just at the completion. Rewards can be anything you like to do. They can be simple and inexpensive, but they should be things that are important to you. Reading for pleasure, relaxing, participating in sports, visiting friends, traveling, going to dinner, and exercising can all be used as rewards.

CHAPTER 13

Decision Making

Making decisions and setting boundaries are the cornerstones of time management. Yet making decisions can be a terrifying experience. The most difficult aspect of some situations is not the individual elements that make up the experience. It is the agony associated with making a choice and risking a mistake, a bad outcome, or loss of other opportunities. Most decisions are small, but the larger ones where more is at stake can be truly painful. How do you feel about decision making? Are you fairly comfortable or does the thought of making decisions stop you dead in your tracks?

You probably face twice as many choices than your grand-parents did, from the major life decisions of where and how to earn a living, to have children, and where to live, to the minor ones of choosing a cereal or deodorant. You make literally hundreds of decisions a week, both small and large. If you have poor decision-making skills, it not only wastes time but increases stress. All the worry and agony that goes along with delaying a decision does not make the problem go away. Being indecisive is not a protection; it can feel safer, but that is a mirage. It has consequences. Often delay only intensifies or increases the seriousness of the situation. That terrible knocking sound in your truck when you accelerate is not magically going to go away; it is only going to get worse. Better to call the mechanic today than wait and have to suffer through the weekend before taking it in for repair.

What do you know about your decision-making style? Are you a Jumper, Worrywart, Researcher, or Avoider? Perhaps you are a mix of several styles?

Jump Right In

Do you make decisions too quickly before you get key information? Are you so fast that you do not make reasoned judgments? Do you make snap choices and then have to live with the unforeseen consequences? For you, getting the decision made and behind you is paramount. Though you are often hailed as decisive, those who must live with the results would more likely say you are rash.

Worry, Worry

Do you agonize over each option and play the "what if" game? Every potential scenario gets a full dose of worry and anxiety. As a result, do decisions take a very long time due to constant reevaluation every few days, weeks, or months? As more time passes and other options present themselves, do you do another entire reanalysis, further delaying a final choice?

Research Unto Death

Do you research or investigate an extraordinary amount? Getting caught up in gathering data can take up so much time that the opportunity itself can vanish before the research is complete. Here is a case where information paralyzes rather than frees. Not all information is pertinent to making an informed decision, yet overresearchers do not make this distinction. One issue opens into another like a tree with many branches. Yet each branch takes you farther away from the main issue.

Avoid and Defer

Do you let someone or something else make the decision for you—whoever yells the loudest or whatever has the earliest deadline? Some Avoiders remain in traditional relationships, because the partner makes all the decisions, or in unsatisfying jobs, hoping things will magically get better.

A roadblock to successful decision making can occur when two people are locked into conflicting positions and neither is able or willing to give ground. In those instances it is helpful to forget the specifics of the issue and think about ways to approach solving the problem.

A couple who started a successful grocery store chain decided to divorce. Each wanted to buy the other out at the lowest possible price. How can a reasonable decision be reached? Here are two strategies: (1) Both could hire accountants. If both accountants disagree on the worth, a third accountant would be hired and his or her valuation would be binding. (2) One spouse could arrive at a fair price and payment terms. The other spouse would get to choose whether to be the buyer or the seller, using the other spouse's prices and terms. The roles can be decided by a coin toss. That way neither knew which side of the table he or she would be on and would therefore set a fair amount.

In cases where making a decision seems impossible, often an outside, more objective viewpoint can shed light on the situation. This may not be your best friend, who could be too close to the situation to be objective, but an acquaintance, relative, business associate, or other person whose judgment you respect.

You can learn to make decisions more quickly and easily. The more confidence you have in your ability to do so, the better.

Things to Consider

Make a distinction between a poor decision and a poor outcome. A decision is the result of a process. An outcome is the result, consequence, or aftermath of a decision. It is possible to make a good, well-reasoned decision and still have a bad outcome for reasons beyond your control. A well-thought-out and researched choice to take a new job in a different city can be a good decision—that is, not hasty or ill-planned. Eight months after the move, your company is purchased in a hostile takeover and you are one of dozens or even hundreds laid off. The decision was sound but the outcome was unpredictable. It is not your fault nor a reflection on the quality of the decision that it did not turn out the way you had anticipated.

ACTION STEPS

Here are a set of steps to take when you are overwhelmed by choices:

STEP 1   Narrow the field. How do you make a choice when there are two dozen competing companies that want to lay your carpet? Begin by narrowing your choices. You might do that by reputation, longevity of the company, or reviews from magazines like *Consumer Reports.*

STEP 2   Eliminate those unheard-of companies, those rated lower than the top ten, or any other factors that are red flags. This will reduce your options to five or six companies, which is a much easier number to manage.

STEP 3   Create a list of questions to ask each company. In this discussion process you will no doubt think of other questions. Revise your list and ask the additional questions. At this point a couple more companies will probably fall by the wayside.

STEP 4   Armed with this information, talk with any friends who have ever had carpet installed and ask them about their experiences. They will share things you might not have thought of such as whether installation is guaranteed and for how long. From this you will probably be able to narrow it to two or three companies with comparable products.

STEP 5   At that point, you may be in a position where any of the three you choose will work well for you. Remember, decisions are not always black and white; sometimes they are simply a choice among many good alternatives.

Tips

- Make decisions in a timely fashion. In many instances, ignoring a problem creates a whole host of other problems. After you have gathered the data, and perhaps slept on it overnight, decide and move forward. Rarely does waiting significantly improve the quality of the decision. Recognize the greater unpleasantness, work, loss of money, time, and stress, not to mention loss of sleep that results from delay.

- Do not agonize over minor decisions. They are still minor with or without the agony. Postponing decisions about small problems generally means that they simply turn into larger ones later.

- Learn when to stop gathering facts. Gather enough information to make a sound decision but not all of the possible information. Some decisions really are affected by time constraints and the extra two weeks, two months, or two years spent searching for the last morsel of data can mean that you have missed the window of opportunity. After talking with friends about buying a car, getting recommendations, and checking consumer reports, you may have sufficient information to make an intelligent buying decision. You need not visit every lot, check every Web site or review all the original research studies on consumer satisfaction.

- Do not seek to find a path that has no risk. It is fruitless. There is no such thing as a completely risk-free decision. A good decision simply minimizes the risk and increases the likelihood of a positive outcome.

- Try studied disregard. The Rule of Three strategy, used by a senior manager, is to ignore problems that will solve themselves or that might never need to be solved. This is how it works: Wait three days on any significant issue. In that period, the problem has either resolved itself or intensified and therefore proved itself worthy of attention.

- Don't make a hasty choice, particularly one that goes against your gut instincts, just to quiet others who are clamoring for a decision.

- Decide to decide. Once you do this, life becomes much more simple. You don't have to think about certain issues or questions again. J. W. Marriott, Jr., Chairman and CEO of Marriott International, says, "Early in life I chose to put my family first, then my church, then my business. There is satisfaction to be had in standing firm against the temptations that come with contemporary life." Deciding to decide is recognizing and accepting that there is only so much you can do or handle intelligently.

SECTION 4

Getting Organized

CHAPTER 14

Organizing Your Home

What is your ideal for a home—is it a calm place to rest from the storm? A mini-exploratorium filled with learning opportunities? A fast-moving, filled-with-laughter adventure? Whatever your answer, you can make your home into an environment that works for you. To do that, you need to eliminate the excess and organize the remainder.

If you live in a 3,500-square-foot house with five bedrooms, four different types of pets, kids, cars with garages, workshops, and hobby rooms, there will be more for you to tackle than for a one-bedroom apartment-dweller. However, it is amazing how quickly stuff accumulates regardless of space availability. And it all requires your time and your energy to maintain. Your possessions also need to be stored, cleaned, and insured. Do you really need three full closets of clothes, four cars in a two-car family, or twenty-seven pairs of shoes? We leave cars worth thousands of dollars in the driveway and save useless things and junk in boxes in the garage. At the point when you spend more time maintaining the things in your life than enjoying the fruits of your labor, something needs to be changed.

Take a few moments to walk around your home. Where are your clutter areas?

- Automobiles
- Kids' rooms and play areas
- Closets
- Office
- Kitchen
- Drawers
- Garages and storage areas
- Laundry area
- Bedrooms
- Family room
- Work or hobby areas

Whatever your challenges, you can make order out of chaos by following these four principles:

1. Divide;
2. Reduce;

3. Remove;

4. Rearrange.

Let's use a home office as an example. A similar process can be used for any area that is cluttered.

1. Divide: Start with a plan to put your office in shape. Divide your work area into sections: your primary desk, your bookcase, credenza, second desk or computer work station, and your files. Organize one area at a time. Decide what information, materials, and supplies you use most frequently. Those should be closest to you, while lesser-used items can be stored elsewhere. Break the cleaning and organizing project into steps that easily fit in with your work schedule.

2. Reduce: Throw out as much as possible. Toss outdated versions of manuals and catalogs, extra copies of documents, information you never use, and papers you did not even know were there. Move information you do not need now but which has historical value to the garage or other storage area. Be ruthless about making save-and-toss decisions. Throw it out if:

   • It is a duplicate;
   • It is no longer relevant;
   • The information is readily available elsewhere;
   • You do not have time to read it.

3. Remove: Many items migrate to areas where they do not belong. Remove and forward those items that belong to someone else or live in another area.

4. Rearrange: Organize the remaining items. Group together items that fall into broad categories, such as

reference manuals, journals and magazines, catalogs, and reports. This will enable you to go to one shelf and quickly find related items.

Anything that stays on your desk must be used frequently. Place knickknacks, family photos, clocks, and souvenirs on a shelf or side table instead of on your desk, where they take up valuable space and create a visual distraction. Limit personal items such as toiletries, a spare pair of shoes, or an umbrella to one special drawer. Such items as a calendar, paper clips, stapler, pens, and pencils can also go into a drawer. By keeping the desk surface as free of clutter as possible, you lessen the probability of losing or misplacing papers and make it easier to focus on high-priority items.

Dealing with Future Events

A useful way to keep track of items you will not need for a few days, weeks, or months is to use a tickler file for the entire family.

A tickler file is a system that manages information, tasks, and activities by date. Make twelve files labeled for each month of the year, January through December. Take another set of files numbered from one to thirty-one for the days of the month. Any item you need in the current month goes inside the folder for the specific date. Tickets for next week's game on the twelfth. Any item required for a future month is filed in the monthly files which are placed at the back of the file drawer or box. If you need to check on the schedule for white water rafting in June and this month is April, file it in the June folder. At the first of every month, distribute the items into the date files.

This is an ideal place for items such as:

• Tickets for cultural and sporting events
• Bills to be mailed
• Invoices
• Directions to events
• Sales flyers
• Letters to be answered
• Sign-ups for summer activities
• Dry cleaning pick-up tags
• Reminders for doctor or dentist's appointments
• Reminders for shots for the pets
• Deposit due dates for events
• Travel itinerary and airline tickets
• Greeting and birthday cards

You must check the file each day. All family members can use the same system. That way, there is one place that each person checks for items.

Straightening the House

Cleaning and keeping a home neat can be a constant source of tension and a never-ending battle. Here is a great method for keeping the house picked up. Joan Craig, a professional organizer, recommends that you keep a box or a basket in each room to collect items that belong elsewhere. This prevents you from having to constantly return items. By teaching everyone to place items that don't belong in the room in a box, straightening up then means distributing the items in the basket.

If you have a large house, distribution of the contents of any container can be done two ways: (1) Carry the container from one room, and distribute the items to their proper locations; or (2) collect all the baskets from each room and take them to a central place, like the dining room table, for sorting. Once sorted, place all items for one room back in a container, take them to the appropriate room, empty the container, and leave the container there.

This is a great plan for keeping the home neat, and it is a simple way to teach children a system for keeping things in order. This method also illustrates to children that they have a responsibility to maintain the family living space; it is not just the responsibility of one overworked parent. Other family members can help in the broad sorting process, which brings everyone together. This is also more interesting and pleasant than having to "clean up your room" by yourself.

One of the greatest benefits of this system is that it limits the areas where lost items can be found. Once everyone is in the habit of putting things that do not belong in a room into the basket, all anyone has to do to find the lost item is to go from room to room looking in each basket.

Things to Consider

The KISS (Keep It Sweet and Simple) principle applies here. Your organizing system need not be an elaborate one, nor cost a lot of money. The easier and the simpler it is the more likely you and other family members are to maintain it.

ACTION STEPS

STEP 1   Choose one area to organize. The one that bothers you or family members the most is a good place to begin. Using the closet as an example:

STEP 2   Analyze what you have. Any items that are duplicates, mismatched, nonfitting, unstylish, or stained beyond hope? Respond accordingly.

STEP 3   Remove any items that should more appropriately be stored elsewhere, such as out-of-season items or heavy outerwear. They can even be stored in rarely used luggage.

STEP 4   Sort by type. Group together all pants, shirts, blouses, skirts, dresses, or formal wear. This helps you determine how much space you actually need.

STEP 5   Determine the best location for remaining items. The most often used items should be in the most accessible drawers and shelves.

STEP 6   Purchase any items you need to finish the process—more or a different type of hangers, shelving materials, or containers.

Tips for Housework and Laundry

- If you can afford it, pay someone to do chores you particularly dislike or are tempted to procrastinate on.

- To keep things under control, try cleaning one room each day.

- In larger households, hang a laundry bag inside each person's closet. It is his or her responsibility to take the filled bag to the laundry area and sort items into marked baskets prelabeled by type of wash load. The bag goes back to the closet door. Completed laundry can go back to the appropriate room, or if there is space, remain in the laundry area for pickup by each person.

- Buy low-maintenance clothes. The fewer special cleaning requirements, the simpler and less expensive your laundry will be.

Tips for Errands and Shopping

- Run errands early in the day. Parking is easier, traffic is less dense, and you are more likely to get prompt service.

- Purchase items that have multiple uses. Single-use items are costly in money, time, and space.

- Buy in bulk. Whether you are getting office supplies, appreciation gifts, or cards, it's more efficient to buy for long-range needs than to frequently run out to buy individual items.

- Use a dry erase board mounted inside a kitchen cabinet for an ongoing grocery list. Erase only after items are purchased.

Tips for the Kitchen and Meal Preparation

- Store items close to the area where they are used: pots, pans, and spatulas close to the stove; silverware, napkins, and placemats near the dining area(s).

- For one-dish meals like eggplant parmesan, make two at a time and freeze one.

- Plan meals one week in advance to reduce last-minute trips to the store.

- Cook big meals two nights a week, eat leftovers two nights, and on Friday splurge with a meal out or delivered.

- Alphabetize spices, if you have and use a large quantity.

Tips for Garages

- Hang tools on a wall with outlines so anyone can easily see where they should be returned.

- Keep a separate area that is closest to the door for all your gardening tools.

- Store things on shelves and off the floor, away from rodents and potential water damage.

Tips for Clothing and Storage

- If an item does not fit, the color isn't right, it goes with nothing else you own, or you never wear it, it is time to give it to a charity, send it to a consignment store, recycle it, or donate it to a nonprofit. The original expense of the item no longer matters; it is now worthless to you.

- Always make sure you have garments that serve multiple uses.

- If you buy a new piece of clothing, find something in your closet that can be tossed or donated to charity. This is a painless way to keep your closet manageable.

- Install dividers in drawers for maintaining supplies and other items. You can customize the dividers to the available space.

- Make an inventory of what you have in an off-site storage facility. It will help you remember and is useful for insurance purposes.

General Organizing Tips

- Keep two files, one for instruction manuals and one for guarantees. Staple the receipt to the guarantee or warranty page. Then when you need to return an item, all the information is handy. Purge periodically for appliances sent to charity.

- Place rosters for activities into a tabbed, labeled binder. Each individual tab for sports activities, membership lists, or PTA keeps pertinent information in one place.

- Label photos with the date and people's names as soon as they are developed.

- If you don't use a tickler system, keep a clipboard by the door. Clip all invitations, commitments, directions, and tickets in chronological order.

- Instead of parking your car at the airport, consider taking a cab, shuttle, or limo. They are more convenient and often less expensive.

- Use checklists to simplify shopping, packing for travel, and entertainment.

- Store little-used items farther away. Even on a shelf, keep the least-used items in the back. Keep those items you use frequently in the front of the storage space.

- Keep a pair of scissors near where you read newspapers and magazines. You can easily clip those articles you wish to save.

- Label everything that contains things: binders, folders, suitcases.

- Carry small personalized return address stickers for many purposes, such as: getting film developed, signing up at registration tables, and updating directories.

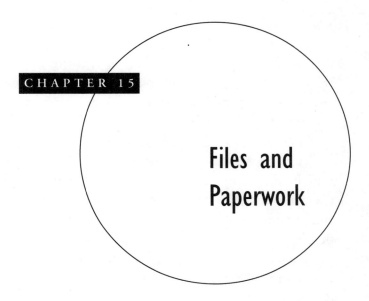

CHAPTER 15

Files and Paperwork

I nformation comes at you from many sources: the phone, fax, voice mail, pagers, e-mail. If it becomes overwhelming, mistakes are made, you feel uncomfortable and out of control, and the stacks of paper get higher and higher. You can even begin to suffer from "CRS"—"Can't Remember Stuff." No, it is not only caused by age. Constant bombardment will have the same effect. Memory dysfunction occurs when you overload yourself and can cause items previously remembered to be dumped. For example, the meeting you just attended ran overtime with no conclusions reached. Once outside the building you now cannot remember a thing the presenter said or where you parked the car. That also accounts for your getting up from your chair for the expressed purpose of getting an item from another room and, once there, having no idea why you dropped by.

How bad is it? Do you find yourself shuffling through stacks of papers on your desk in search of a document you were holding only a moment ago? Are you at a loss to find a place to put all the memos, reports, and correspondence that comes your way? And do you ever wonder where you filed that important letter? It becomes increasingly difficult to find things, keep track of projects, or work comfortably when the stacks and piles turn into clutter. If you do not move that paper, you may never see your desktop again. Whether you are in a home-based business, a fast-paced start-up endeavor, a corporate setting, or just trying to keep up with home-related activities, you are faced with a paperwork explosion.

The solution is to take control: Get organized up front, maintain that organization, and create a filing system that works. Ensuring a smooth paper flow means removing the stacks, rearranging and color-coding files, and learning to handle the in- and out-baskets quickly and effectively.

The In-Basket

Ideally, the in-basket is the one place for new information and a location where other people put material they want you to see. It is an essential tool, but you have to learn to use it correctly. Do not try to transform it into a filing system, a bulletin board, or a nagging reminder. Your in-basket isn't working if:

- You don't have one. New information is likely to be scattered anywhere throughout your home or office.
- You have one, and even though you sort through it many times a day, the stack never gets smaller.
- You only touch your in-basket when papers threaten to cascade to the floor.
- The entire top of your desk or the dining room table *is* the in-basket.
- Your coworkers know the only way to make sure you see something is to put it on your chair.

At work, you should sort through and handle the papers in your in-basket twice a day. At home, twice a week should be sufficient, particularly if junk mail never reaches your desk. Sort your mail while standing over the trash can. Place junk mail in the trash without bothering to open it. Establish a To Do list and a Reading file. With these two items, it should take no more than fifteen minutes to empty your in-basket. Make a decision on every piece of paper and put it in its proper location—not at the bottom of the basket!

Papers relating to a project you are currently working on should be quickly scanned and put in the file for that project. The latest in-house periodical, a newsletter, or long memo all go in the Reading file. Children's school papers go into their activities binder. Something requiring your signature should be signed immediately and put in the out-basket or by the front door for mailing. Throw away the draft of the third revision that supersedes the second revision which is to be followed by the semifinal copy.

Handling the in-basket means sorting, filing, delegating, and tracking its contents. It does not necessarily mean completing the work on every item. Projects that require your further attention need temporary homes until you have the time to work on them. Each time you file a piece of paper that requires additional action on your part, make a note on your To Do list. This eliminates the fear that once it is filed away and out of sight, it will be permanently forgotten.

Those items that need more than a couple of minutes to read should go into a Reading file. If you take the time to read everything when it first arrives, you will never get through your in-basket. Scan and save only the material that you are likely to read in depth. Scheduling thirty minutes twice a week should be enough to keep you current and the reading stack down. Take reading along to look over while you wait for appointments or while commuting or traveling. When your Reading file is full, sort the oldest portion with this question in mind, "How likely am I to read this or refer to the information in the near future?" Then respond accordingly. You will find yourself tossing much of it.

To help decide what is worth your saving to review later, keep these guidelines in mind. Realize your limitations. Decide what kind of information is essential to what you do and the way you live. Focus on information that helps you see the big picture. How does this help you do your job better? How does this fit in with your new marketing efforts? Do not try to absorb everything. Just because an item is interesting is not good enough. Will you use it again in the next three months? If not, pass it by.

Immediately relate new ideas or concepts to something else you already know. Find a connection to anchor the information to the real world. Think of adding onto a house. The foundation is what you know now. Attach each new idea to some part of the building you are constructing. Give yourself permission to let go of all the stuff you could possibly know or that it would be nice to know. Concentrate on truly understanding that which you read and anchoring it to events, concepts, and tasks that you face regularly. And the next time someone asks whether you have read the latest best-seller and you start to hyperventilate, just think, is he or she as busy as you are? If so, they probably have not read it either.

Controlling the volume of paper is the first step to personal organization. Beware of creeping clutter that is most often caused by being away for a few days, suddenly hitting a busy cycle, or the onset of a crisis. No excuses, take the few minutes required to go through the stacks. Most of it will go "out" again immediately.

Filing It and Finding It Again

How long has your "To File" pile been sitting there, calling for attention? Are the items at the bottom old enough to be considered archives? Have you needed something that you could not put your hands on quickly? If you have a home office, keep your business and personal files separate. This prevents family members from possibly mixing up client projects as they sort through papers looking for the local swimming pool schedule.

Start your file management project by creating working project files. These may be client or customer files, key projects, committees, or contracts. Another main category will contain your ongoing operational files that deal with administrative activities. These can include budget, newsletters,

travel, vendors, and staff meetings. If you have a third component to your job, create a section for those as well. The goal
is to have a few—not more than four—broad areas. Each section represents a logical division and should contain a number of individual files.

Label each file with a broad heading that covers all the
papers inside. Use nouns for file headings. For example,
"Mailing List," "Warranties," "Insurance," "Printing,"
"Correspondence," "Investments," and "Newsletters." Broad
categories allow for flexibility. Avoid starting a label with an
adjective, such as *the* or *an,* or using a number. When trying
to retrieve a document you will think first of what it concerns, not the date it took place.

Sort your files by use. If you touch them every three to
four weeks, they can remain close to you. If you use them less
often, banish them to your unit's central filing system or at
home to the file cabinets located in the basement or storage
facility. Keep in mind that a study by Stanford University
found that 87 percent of filed paper is never looked at again.

Paper should serve as a means to an end. Records, documents, and information are only useful if they are easily
retrievable. Keeping up with the filing and filing only important things will make your life much easier.

Things to Consider

Paper usually represents information, and a large percentage of
information has value for only a limited time. Hoarding—
whether in stacks or in files—does not prevent the aging
process. Eventually you end up keeping worthless information.

ACTION STEPS

STEP 1   Divide your files into three categories: "To Stay," "To Toss," and "To Store Elsewhere."

STEP 2   Label the files that will remain. Choose the broadest possible categories. Thick files are easier to deal with than thin. Consolidate all related materials under the most general category that is practical.

STEP 3   Label all files with a noun. Find a key subject area and use that to label the file. A more effective label than "How to Negotiate Contracts" is "Contract Negotiation."

STEP 4   Add any loose papers from your desktop into your files. Jot a note on your To Do list if they require action.

STEP 5   Divide your individually labeled files into broad categories, such as: "Family Finances," "Children's Activities," "Business Expenses." Then alphabetize within each grouping to make retrieval smooth and easy.

STEP 6   Purge the files going to storage. Remove notes, duplicates, and information that is no longer useful. Staple all related papers and remove clips which easily fall off.

Tips on Paper Management

- Decide what to do with each piece of paper the first time you touch it, and put it away immediately. If you have the time to put it in a pile, you have time to file it.

- Keep only one project or file open on your desk at any time. This reduces the likelihood of stray papers becoming attached to the incorrect document and misfiled.

- Clear your desk at the end of each day, no matter what. Schedule a few minutes to do so.

- When taking notes, write information on the correct document the first time, not on little pieces of paper, which are easily lost.

- Limit your reading material. Realize that you cannot read or retain all the information that you receive. A good rule of thumb is to save items that you plan to use within three months.

- When unsure about a document, ask yourself, "What would I do if it were one week before vacation?" Act accordingly.

- With each piece of paper, ask, "What's the worst thing that could happen if I threw this away?" Unless the outcome is critical, toss it!

- If you have magazines in good condition, consider donating them to nursing homes, schools, hospitals, and clinics or anywhere people have to wait for a period of time. Some local nonprofit organizations may appreciate them.

- If you have not read the last four issues of a magazine, it is time to end your subscription.

• Eliminate the junk mail you receive by writing to Direct Marketing Association, Mail Preference Service, P.O. Box 9008, Farmingdale, New York 11735-9008. Include your full name and address, and request that your name be removed from their mailing list.

Tips on Filing

• Avoid nonspecific file labels, such as "General," "Miscellaneous," "Overall Information," or "Pending." They are traps for loose paper.

• Keep extra file folders close at hand. Create a new file as soon as you get paper related to a new project.

• Place the most recent document in the front of the file. This habit will save you much searching time.

• Resist the impulse to copy papers and place them in different files. Place papers in the category most likely to come to mind when you think of the subject.

• Maintain your filing system. Remember to file regularly. Backlogs become procrastination traps.

• Do not bother to keep every business card you receive, information you already have in another form, duplicates, or items other people simply insist you take.

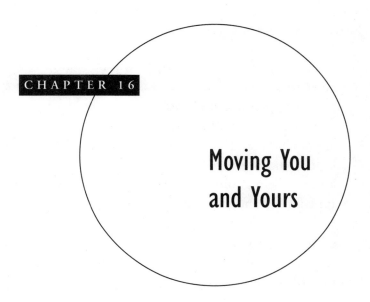

CHAPTER 16

Moving You and Yours

For most people, moving is a least-favorite activity. Whether you are moving across country or across town, the amount of effort is the same. Each and every object must be wrapped and boxed. If you have had the experience of cleaning out the house of a parent or other relative, you are familiar with the amount of effort and emotional distress that accompanies such a task. Even when you are moving by choice—a promotion or marriage that takes you across the country—it is an emotionally charged time. However, there are ways to make the experience bearable.

Once you decide to go, you will be swamped with ideas, concerns, and needs that will instantly spring to mind. As you talk to friends and associates to share the news, they too will have ideas. Write them all down. After the initial burst of anticipation and excitement (or dread), take a three-ring binder and organize these thoughts into categories. Tasks to be done before, during, and after the move will have separate time frames and will need to be handled accordingly. Identify special areas that will require attention throughout the move, such as your children's needs and demands. This is the first step in creating order out of the seemingly insurmountable number of things to do.

Before the Move

Preplanning is the most important part of an efficient and smooth moving experience. It is a major undertaking, so treat it as you would any large project. Start planning at least two months before your move date. Everyone in the family should have a role in the effort. Post a large wall calendar where everyone can see it. Assign completion dates to each of the items in your binder and transfer them to the calendar. This helps keep everyone focused on what has to be done, by when, and by whom.

Have a layout plan for your new location. A floor plan of the new home or apartment will help you visualize how your belongings will fit. You will need some kind of organizational chart that includes a list of your furnishings and a notation about which room they will go to. It will help the mover place items properly, and if the mover turns out to be all of your friends, it prevents you from being pulled in eight directions at once with questions about "Where does this go?"

Begin collecting boxes far in advance of the move. You will need an incredible number of them. Liquor boxes are a good all-around, all-purpose-size box, as are the boxes in which copy paper is delivered. You can also use heavy-duty moving boxes. Avoid damaged or tired boxes that may not hold up during the move and can cause spillage, breakage, or other damage to your goods. An average three-bedroom house will require between seventy and 100 boxes.

If you choose to hire professional movers, they can do the packing for you, along with transportation and unloading. Some will even unpack at your destination. These options are limited only by your budget. If you choose to work with a moving company, be clear about your expectations and be sure to read the fine print on your contract. There are two main complaints about moving companies. One is timeliness and the other is damage to your goods. Ask for references. Explain your timetable. If your interactions prior to the move date are less than stellar, it bodes ill for the actual move. Find another company.

Be sure you read and understand the liability of the company in the event that they damage your possessions. Most contracts do not replace dollar-for-dollar—forty to sixty cents on the dollar is more common. Additional coverage can be purchased from the mover, generally at a high cost. One option is to find out if your homeowner's insurance has a policy rider that covers moves. Compare the cost and coverage allowances with what your mover can provide.

Don't make the mistake of undervaluing your own time, energy, and resources. Consider how much of your time will be spent running around to locate boxes, packing materials, and small truck rentals. Include the cost of gas for your vehicle, as well as your labor in packing the boxes, loading, and transporting them on both ends of the move. It may be worth your time and money to hire specialists. If budget is a problem, get assistance for portions of the move to relieve some of the load.

Packing

This is the ideal time to sort and throw away those items you don't want, need, or use any longer. Even if you have been simplifying and reducing the amount of stuff you own, there is nothing like a move to encourage even greater reduction and spur decision making.

The selection of packing materials is very important. Many of us still think of packing and newspapers in the same breath. Newspapers are great for filling up space in boxes and for certain items. However, it can also stain items and leave fingerprints on the nice white paint in your new home. Use plain wrapping paper, bubble wrap, or foam.

Purchase all the additional packing materials you will need, such as sealing tape and large marking pens. Buy wide, heavy-duty masking and strapping tape for sealing boxes. Thin, inexpensive tape can quickly produce frustrating tangles when unrolling from the dispenser. When labeling boxes, write legibly in large letters. Have at least five black marking pens. As you move from room to room you will set one down and not find it for hours. Do not spend precious time trying to locate it.

This is an excellent time to invest in a large packing tape dispenser with a cutting edge, to make the job of sealing boxes go much faster than it would take using a pair of scissors. Aprons with pockets work wonderfully to keep small items handy.

Use small boxes for heavy things like books and records. For lighter items, consider packing three or four smaller ones into a single larger container. This serves as added protection while saving time and effort during the move. Very large boxes are good if you fill them with padding for paintings and wall hangings. They are similarly good for large, bulky, and lightweight items like linen or blankets. Use care in packing large boxes; they can easily become too heavy.

Organize your packing room by room. Start with those items used least often. First pack items that are primarily used to decorate or enhance the look of a room. Their absence will not cause inconvenience. Items that fall into this category include books (except those few you may read between now and moving day), paintings, posters, knickknacks, artwork, hobbies, and collections. Move slowly inward in concentric circles toward the most frequently used items.

Label every box with room location and the general category of contents (no more than ten words). Number each box on the label and enter that number on a master log of boxes. On the master log, list the detailed contents of each box. (This step may seem unnecessary but it will save much confusion when the boxes arrive at your new address.)

If you have a large collection of similar items, a more specific label is needed. This helps during unpacking by alerting you to the best order to unpack. For example, if you have forty-seven boxes of cooking items, the everyday eating dishes will be needed sooner than the silver chafing dish. If you will need the computer books immediately, separate them from the general fiction, science fiction, mysteries, and biographies.

Label each room so the movers—be they friends or professionals—know where to place items. If practical, go to your new home on the day before the move with a good supply of paper and tape. In plain sight, label each room number one, number two, number three or by usage (library, den, sunroom). If you have firm feelings about furniture locations, label the walls. Painters' tape may be used to avoid damage to walls and woodwork.

Keeping Sane

There is nothing as exhausting—physically, mentally, and emotionally—as moving. Make your life as easy as possible. Be prepared for extra stress and the resulting short tempers. To make things easier, budget for eating out more often or having meals delivered. If you enjoy cooking, cook ahead and freeze full meals. In this way, dinner decisions are eliminated and become one less thing to worry about. Keep your priorities in order. A successful move means that it is done in the time frame you have set and the end result is a new home, not a nervous breakdown.

As you get closer to the move date, make special arrangements for your pets and children. The house has already been disrupted, things are strewn about, the last thing you need is a child underfoot asking about every item as it goes into the box. This is a great time for relatives to take your children for a visit, some time out with friends, or some fun activity that takes the children out from underfoot. These options are fun and will not be seen as the punishment that "Go to your room and get out of my hair" would be.

Even if you are moving to the home of your dreams, moving is tiring. Don't push so hard that you increase the load. Take frequent breaks. Treat yourself to dinner, a hot bath, a massage, or anything that will make you feel better.

Protect your back. Even if you hire movers, you will be amazed how often you must bend and stoop during a move. Give your back extra support during both packing and unpacking. Practice good body mechanics when you pick things up by bending your knees and keeping your back straight. You can get a good back brace from your chiropractor or from a store that sells medical supplies.

Get help from your friends. They can help pack or gather boxes, particularly if they work at a large company that receives many daily deliveries. Look to them for assistance in planning, cooking, baby-sitting, and hand-holding. When the move, the dust, and the boxes begin to get to you, take a break and eat out with a buddy.

Despite all your best planning, things will go wrong. Everything takes longer than you expect, and glitches are bound to happen. Try not to let it make you crazy. Expect something to either slip up or slip through the cracks.

The Last Thing

Leave at least one entire day for an apartment and two days for a house for clean-up and a final walk-through. When you go through the house, open every cupboard door and drawer. Even if you are positive it is empty, look again.

Take a stepladder so you can climb up to see all the way to the back of the last shelf. That is where some little item has been overlooked. Bring two large bags with you, one for trash and one for last-minute items. Even in an empty house, the final walk-through will take longer than you think.

Upon Arrival

When you arrive and are unpacking, particularly the first day, pets should be put in a quiet room in the new location or a kennel until the movers have left. The move was stressful enough, and all the activity and the new location will often make pets frantic. Give them food and water, and visit with them often to provide reassurance. Children, too, will be concerned, excited, and maybe even a little frightened. If you are moving close to anyone whom you know, ask an adult to spend time with the child; it will smooth the transition.

Use your garage or spare bedroom to store nonessential boxes and items. Be sure to stack boxes with the labels facing outward. Unpacking takes time, even if done in an organized fashion. It's important to have some livable space during this potentially overwhelming process.

Recycle all your packing materials. Keep large plastic garbage bags on hand to collect the packing debris. Sort the crumpled paper, bubble wrap, and packing peanuts. Break down the boxes and bundle them for recycling. Arrange for curbside pickup or plan a trip to a recycling center.

General Moving Checklist

Make a flowchart for the weeks preceding the move.

Eight weeks before:

• Contact moving companies to get estimates. Contact your homeowner's insurance company about coverage.

• Start collecting boxes.

• Notify magazine and catalog companies of your address change.

Six weeks before:

• Arrange to get school records transferred.

• Begin packing areas not frequently used like the basement, attic, and out-of-season clothes. Packing a few boxes each day will make the process seem less overwhelming.

• Discard, sell, consign, or give away unused belongings.

• Contact utility companies for shut-off and start-up times.

Four weeks before:

• Return all borrowed items and collect items loaned.

• Get copies of medical, dental, birth, and pet immunization records.

• Make hotel and travel arrangements for the family.

• Contact the post office in your new city.

• Send change-of-address forms to insurance companies, Department of Motor Vehicles, etc.

Two weeks before:

• Check with local authorities at both ends of your trip about regulations on large vehicles, loading constraints, or other access limitations. If you will need a dumpster, learn the requirements.

• Arrange for storage facilities if necessary.

• Return library books.

• Have the car serviced.

• Transfer club affiliations.

• Arrange for work that has to be done at the new home.

• Cook and freeze extra meals.

One week before:

• Do intensive packing.

• Arrange for connecting or disconnecting utilities, telephone, cable, water, garbage, and other services.

• Make plans for children and pets on moving day.

• Transfer bank, stocks, and safety deposit box.

Things to Consider

No matter your feelings, this too will pass. Focus on the end result.

Tips

• Plan your move to fall on any day between Sunday and Thursday. It is less expensive and service providers are less rushed. Rental truck availability is greater.

- Pack business and personal essentials separately for minimal confusion.

- If you do not use a wardrobe box and are moving across town, keep your clothes on hangers and lay them on the backseat of the car. Transfer them directly into the closets. This is an ideal assignment for one person.

- Pack one or two boxes with essentials: one set of linens, a towel, medication, a favorite child's toy, toilet paper, extra glasses, soap. Choose the bare essentials that you will need for a couple of days while you concentrate on the heavy unpacking. Keep an "Important Box" with keys, checks, moving receipts, agreements, checklists close to hand.

- No phone number is considered yours until the service is actually turned on. Wait to print your letterhead, stationery, envelopes, and business cards. The phone company is not liable or responsible for financial losses caused by changes to phone numbers, even promised ones.

- Consider hiring a service that specializes in unpacking or organizing. These are listed in the phone book under "Moving Services—Labor and Materials."

- Be prepared to live in and around boxes longer than you anticipated.

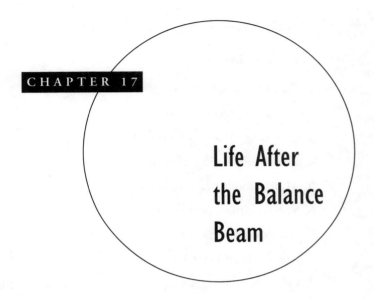

CHAPTER 17

Life After the Balance Beam

A quiet revolution is taking place. More and more younger workers are telling employers that family and personal needs are paramount. They are even willing to make adjustments in the financial arena to live more balanced lives. As you work through this book and make changes in your life, people around you will notice the differences. As you continue this process, talk to others about how they have simplified their lives. There are many kindred spirits out there for you to meet and in turn help guide. Simplifying is an ongoing process that requires your regular attention. Some of the benefits you will receive and changes you will notice include:

1. Relief from unnecessary tension and worry;

2. Fewer unnecessary hassles;

3. Improved quality of interpersonal interactions;

4. Better scheduling of time;

5. More time for leisure activities;

6. Enhanced job performance;

7. Greater appreciation of the present situation;

8. Less guilt and stress;

9. Less "analysis paralysis" and faster decision making;

10. Greater enthusiasm for work and life in general;

11. A more fulfilling life;

12. Peace of mind.

Keep these final tenets in mind as you continue on your road to a simpler and more satisfying life:

- Your first obligation is to look out for yourself, your interests, and your priorities. No one will do this for you.

- Keep your job and your life in perspective. Success at the expense of relaxation and enjoyment is no success.

- Put pride in its correct place. Be proud that you found time for a break and still got done what needed to be done. Do not be proud because you have not enjoyed a weekend break in three months.

- Take yourself less seriously. Learn to see and appreciate the lighter side of life.

• Learn when to say "No." Be firm without apology, undue explanation, or guilt.

• Simplify in every way. For a life worth living, eliminate the unimportant, whether it be relationships, tasks, responsibilities, possessions, or beliefs.

All the best to you.

Afterword

The ongoing theme of my work as a professional organizer for the past twenty years has been, "Clutter is postponed decisions." Sometimes the clutter is physical—overstuffed closets and desk piled high, but often it is mental—good intentions abandoned and important obligations ignored. We are left feeling stressed and guilty. Odette Pollar's book, *Take Back Your Life,* is a practical guide for helping you make decisions about how to live your life.

It is embarrassing to admit, but when I first began my career as a professional organizer, I actually believed that if I were just organized enough, I could do everything I wanted. I soon realized the folly of that premise! A creative mind always has more ideas than the physical body can carry out. One of my roles as a professional organizer is to assist clients in making choices about which ideas to implement, which to delegate, and which to eliminate.

Take Back Your Life can serve as your personal guide for making decisions that will enhance the quality of your personal and professional lives. Eliminating physical and mental clutter is an ongoing challenge. New opportunities arise, and we forget we need to let go of something old to make room for the new—or even to ignore the new to keep the best of the old!

Put this book where you can refer to it often. Make a note in your calendar to read Odette's final chapter "Life After the

Balance Beam" once a month, review your own decision—
and live happily ever after!

—Barbara Hemphill,
author of *Taming the Paper Tiger*

Resources

Organizing

Aslett, Don. *Clutter Free! Finally & Forever.* Pocatello, ID: Marsh Creek Press, 1995.

Eisenberg, Ronni, with Kate Kelly. *Organize Yourself!* New York: Collier Books, MacMillian Publishing Company, 1986.

Hemphill, Barbara. *Taming the Office Tiger.* Washington, DC: Kiplinger Books, 1996.

———. *Taming the Paper Tiger: Organizing the Paper in Your Life.* New York: Dodd, Mead & Company, 1998.

Kanarek, Lisa. *Organizing Your Home Office for Success.* New York: Plume Books, 1993.

Lehmkuhl, Dorothy, and Dolores Lamping. *Organizing for the Creative Person.* New York: Crown Paperbacks, 1993.

Lively, Lynn. *Managing Information Overload.* New York: AMACOM, 1996.

Pollar, Odette. *Organizing Your Workspace: A Guide to Personal Productivity.* Menlo Park, CA: Crisp Publications, Inc., 1999.

Silver, Susan. *Organized to Be the Best!* Los Angeles: Adams-Hall Publishing, 1991.

Balance and Simplification

Babbit, Dave, and Kathy Babbit. *Downscaling: Simplify and Enrich Your Lifestyle.* Chicago: Moody Press, 1993.

Hochschild, Arlie Russell. *The Time Bind: When Work Becomes Home and Home Becomes Work.* New York: Metropolitan Books, Henry Holt and Company, 1997.

Kirsch, M. M. *How to Get Off the Fast Track and Live a Life that Money Can't Buy.* Los Angeles: Lowell House, 1991.

Leider, Richard J., and David A. Shapiro. *Repacking Your Bags.* San Francisco: Berrett-Koehler Publishers, 1995.

Levine, Karen. *Keeping Life Simple: 7 Guiding Principles, 500 Tips and Ideas.* Pownal, VT: Storey Publishing, 1996.

Lizotte, Ken, and Barbara A. Litwak. *Balancing Work and Family.* New York: AMACOM, 1995.

Magid, Renée Y., Ph.D., and Melissa M. Codkind, M.H.A. . *Work and Personal Life: Managing the Issues.* Menlo Park, CA: Crisp Publications, 1995.

McGinnis, Alan Loy. *The Balanced Life.* Minneapolis: MN: Augsburg Fortress, 1997.

O'Neil, John R. *The Paradox of Success: When Winning at Work Means Losing at Life.* New York: G. P. Putnam's Sons, 1993.

Pollar, Odette. *365 Ways to Simplify Your Work Life.* Chicago: Dearborn Financial Publishing, Inc., 1996.

St. James, Elaine. *Simplify Your Life: 100 Ways to Slow Down and Enjoy the Things that Really Matter.* New York: Hyperion, 1994.

Time Management

Culp, Stephanie. *You Can Find More Time for Yourself Every Day.* Cincinatti, OH: Betterway Books, 1994.

Klein, Ruth. *Where Did the Time Go: The Working Woman's Guide to Creative Time Management.* Rocklin, CA: Prima Publishing, 1994.

Mallinger, Allan E., M.D., and Jeannette DeWyze. *Too Perfect: When Being in Control Gets Out of Control.* New York: Clarkson N. Potter, Inc., 1992.

Morrisey, George L. *Creating Your Future: Personal Strategic Planning for Professionals.* San Francisco: Berrett-Koehler Publishers, 1992.

Morrisey, George L. *Getting Your Act Together: Goal Setting for Fun, Health and Profit.* Reading, MA: Addison-Wesley Publishing Co., 1980.

Peisner, Paula. *Finding Time: Breathing Space for Women Who Do Too Much.* Naperville, IL.: Sourcebook Trade, 1992.

Raber, Merrill F., MSW, Ph.D., and George Dyck, M.D. *Managing Stress for Mental Fitness.* Menlo Park, CA: Crisp Publications, 1987.

Work and Family

Laqueur, Maria, and Donna Dickinson. *Breaking Out of 9 to 5: How to Redesign Your Job to Fit You.* Princeton, NJ: Petersons Guides, n.d.

Lee, Deborah. *Having It All, Having Enough: How to Create a Career/Family Balance That Works for You.* New York: AMACOM, 1996.

Levine, James, and Todd Pittinsky. *Working Fathers: New Strategies for Balancing Work and Family.* Reading, MA: Addison-Wesley Publishing Co., 1997.

Murray, Katherine. *The Working Parents' Handbook: How to Succeed at Work, Raise Your Kids, Maintain a Home, and Still Have Time for You.* Indianapolis, IN: JIST Works, 1996.

Peel, Kathy. *The Family Manager's Guide for Working Moms.* New York: Ballantine Books, 1997.

Price, Susan Crites, and Tom Price. *The Working Parents Help Book: Practical Advice for Dealing With the Day-to-Day Challenges of Kids and Careers.* Princeton, NJ: Petersons Guides, 1996.

For More Information and Assistance

The National Association of Professional Organizers
1033 La Posada Drive, Suite 220
Austin, Texas 78752-3880
(512) 454-8626
Information and Referral Line: (512) 206-0151
Fax: (512) 454-3036
E-mail: napo@assnmgmt.com
http://www.napo.net

Acknowledgments

My appreciation to all of my clients who have been so willing to share their experiences and who are actively engaged in simplifying and balancing their lives.

My sincere thanks to Katrina Brabham, Tom Nevermann, Kim Moeller, and Mary Ann Pollar for reading with a critical eye. Karen Rossum deserves special thanks for all of her suggestions, ideas, and constant support. My thanks also to Jean Mayeda for manuscript preparation and editing.

About the Author

Odette Pollar is a nationally recognized author, trainer, speaker, and productivity expert who directs Time Management Systems in Oakland, California. Pollar travels nationally, consulting and delivering programs that enhance performance, improve office management, and streamline day-to-day operations.

Pollar writes the nationally syndicated newspaper column "Smart Ways to Work." She is a frequent radio and television guest, discussing workplace issues.

Pollar is the author of *Organizing Your Workspace: A Guide to Personal Productivity* (Crisp Publications, 1992), *Dynamics of Diversity: Strategic Programs for Your Organization* (Crisp Publications, 1994), and *365 Ways to Simplify Your Work Life* (Dearborn Financial Publishing, 1996).

Pollar has worked in public and private agencies, corporations, and professional associations. She founded TMS in 1979 and uses her eighteen years' experience as a management consultant, writer, and entrepreneur in her consulting work, teaching professionals easy, effective ways to manage time, track projects and activities, balance work/life issues, simplify paperwork, and streamline work flow. Her corporate clients include Levi Strauss, McDonald's, Hewlett-Packard, Shell Oil, VISA, and Pacific Bell.

Your Feedback

I want to hear from you. Please write me with your feelings about this book, as well as any suggestions or comments. I am particularly interested in your experiences and in the results you receive from using the ideas in this book.

1. This is what I liked and found helpful about the book:

_____

_____

_____

_____

_____

2. These are the specific suggestions I used and the results:

_____

_____

_____

_____

_____

3. Here are some suggestions for change or improvements:

_____

_____

_____

_____

_____

Want to share your ideas with others? Let me know...

The idea(s) I have used to simplify and/or balance my life

include: _____

_____

_____

_____

_____

Here's how to communicate with Odette. Write to Odette Pollar, Time Management Systems, 1441 Franklin Street, Suite 301, Oakland, CA 94612 e-mail: opollartms@aol.com

I am interested in (check all that apply):

_____ Keynote speeches

_____ Training and seminars

_____ Personal improvement products

_____ An individual consultation

(Please attach a business card)